Asclepius

ASCLEPIUS

The Perfect Discourse of Hermes Trismegistus

edited and translated by

Clement Salaman

Duckworth

This impression 2009
First published in 2007 by
Gerald Duckworth & Co. Ltd.
90-93 Cowcross Street, London EC1M 6BF
Tel: 020 7490 7300
Fax: 020 7490 0080
info@duckworth-publishers.co.uk
www.ducknet.co.uk

A catalogue record for this book is available
from the British Library

ISBN 978 0 7156 3564 3

Typeset by Ray Davies

Contents

Acknowledgements

I would like to thank all those who have assisted in the preparation of this book. There are friends who have given particularly valuable help and whom I would like to mention by name. First of all I must mention my wife, Juliet, without whose encouragement and toil (at times painful!) this book would not have appeared. I am also extremely grateful to Arthur Farndell for many major improvements in the text and introduction, to Valery Rees for detailed help on the notes and useful suggestions on subjects needing to be covered, and to Dr Joseph Milne for profound insights into the early Christian Church and for the suggestion that a passage on Dionysius should be included in the Introduction. I am also grateful to Dr Jeremy Naydler for inspiring this translation and finding time during an extremely busy period to answer questions for me on Ancient Egypt, and for making many useful suggestions on the Introduction and Translation. I must thank Jill Line for useful comments on the Introduction and above all for compiling the Index. Dr Angela Voss has been of great help to me in drawing attention to passages from St Augustine and St Thomas Aquinas and also to her own paper, 'From Allegory to Anagoge: The Question of Symbolic Perception in a Literal World'. I would also like to thank Geoffrey Pearce and Bruce Ramell for their comments on astronomy and music respectively, and Anna McLelland for spending many hours helping me to revise the translation. Susan Gandar has drawn my attention to the importance of the work of King Alphonso X of Castile, for which I an grateful. A big penultimate note: I do wish to record enormous gratitude to my daughter-in-law Prabh for rescuing my wife and myself from drowning in a sea of 'computery' while composing the final draft. Last, but by no means least, I would like to record my debt to the late Joan Crammond who devotedly typed the first drafts of the translation.

List of Illustrations

Introduction

The *Asclepius*, together with its sister book, the *Corpus Hermeticum*, contains the philosophic wisdom ascribed in ancient times to the Egyptian god Thoth (or Tehuti), who was said by St Augustine (354-430 AD) to have lived on earth at the same time as Moses. The Greek original (now lost) of the Latin text from which this book was translated, was probably composed between 100 and 300 AD in Alexandria. The earliest record of our Latin version is the use of it by St Augustine for quotation.

The original title of *Asclepius* was *Logos teleios,* 'the perfect discourse'. Why that title? The author said that it had 'more divine power than any I have previously spoken'. It seems to express his deepest thoughts on the Oneness of the universe and the true, divine nature of Man. 'Hermes' influenced early Christianity and has inspired some of the greatest thinkers in the West from Dionysius, through Isaac Newton (who translated the Hermetic *Emerald Tablet*), to Ralph Waldo Emerson.

The setting

The opening of the *Asclepius* creates an atmosphere of intense fervour and expectation. The setting is Egyptian, but the emotion is universal. It is one where disciples wait expectantly to hear mysterious secrets from their teacher which they hope will transform their lives. The master is insistent upon secrecy. No one is allowed to hear the conversation except three special disciples: Asclepius, Tat and Hammon. Asclepius' name was famous, for his grandfather was the first outstanding doctor of antiquity and was made a god after his death. He was honoured in Greece and Rome as well as in Egypt. His grandson was now devoting himself to the wise Hermes to study philosophy, the art of healing the soul. Hammon's late entry to the select company is to emphasise that only the suitably prepared may be admitted to the circle, for 'a conversation worthy of such reverence and on such a profound topic would be profaned by the arrival and presence of many people'.[1] Jesus shows similar concern to protect his teaching: 'Give not that which is holy to the dogs, neither cast ye your pearls before swine, lest they trample them under their feet, and turn again and rend you.'[2]

There is another consideration. A conversation is two-way. What the teacher can say, and from what part of his mind the instruction comes, is dependent upon the state of the audience. Hermes points out a number of times the very concentrated attention and total receptivity required. The presence of this state is referred to at the beginning of the work: 'When Hammon had entered the sanctuary, and the fervour of the four men had filled this holy place, in due silence the minds and hearts of all hung upon the lips of Hermes, and divine love began to speak.'[3] The intimation is that the inner silence and fervour of the four men were necessary for the revelation of divine love.

And what is it that divine love reveals? Ultimately that the apparent multiplicity is in fact a unity. 'The elements, then, by which the whole world has been formed are four: fire, water, earth, air.' But Hermes also states, 'The world is one, the soul is one, God is one.'[4] This paradox appears a number of times in different forms throughout the *Asclepius*. It cannot be unravelled by the ordinary mind, except in a theoretical and misleading way. The real unravelling takes place only in experience; or perhaps in the realisation that there is no mystery to unravel. This experience is not at all like the acquiring of facts from a book or lecture. The knowledge really comes from within, but its effect is to show that in reality there is no within and no without. It is a dramatic, instant transformation of the viewpoint from which everything is apprehended and experienced. There are no boundaries. 'The knowledge of God', says Hermes 'is to be attained by a godlike concentration of consciousness.' It 'comes like a rushing river tumbling in flux from above to the depths beneath'.[5]

Hermetic cosmology

The universe which Hermes presents to us is hierarchical and governed by the law of the supreme or first God. He is linked to corporeal matter by a chain of being, yet He himself is also in every link, and this chain is all ultimately held in love. The administrator of all things is the Cosmos, described by Hermes as the second god. Then come the celestial gods, followed by the daemons, their attendant spirits. From the gods and daemons 'continual influences are borne throughout the world'.[6] The character and state of every body is determined by these influences. Human beings come next and then living creatures who have a soul, after these the vegetable kingdom, beings without a soul. Finally, there is inert matter.

The forms of all beings belong to classes (generally referred to as archetypes in the Translation). The forms have endless variety, yet each individual is instantly recognisable as belonging to its class. Hermes perhaps suggests that the forms are an example of the many, and that the class (or archetype) represents the One. The forms (except for those of the gods) are mortal, yet the classes are immortal and therefore in a realm beyond sense.

Thus the fundamental principle of Hermes' cosmology is that the manifest, moving and perishable is governed by the unmanifest, unmoving and imperishable. Ultimately this is unmoving consciousness. Hermes says of consciousness that 'in its totality, being similar to divinity, … (it) is itself motionless. Yet it is self-moving within its own stillness. Consciousness is holy, uncorrupt and eternal and whatever can be named higher than that, if anything can be.'[7]

In discussing eternity and stillness Hermes comes closest to explaining the enigma of how the supreme God can be both one and all. He states that time always turns upon itself and thus always returns to eternity. The idea of turning on itself suggests the movement of the heavenly bodies which in time always return to the same positions: they are never out of positions which they have been in countless times before and in which they will be countless times again. Thus there is a movement in eternity which is always within itself. 'The stillness of eternity is in movement'. But 'the movement of time is made still by the unchanging law which governs its course'.[8] The concept is of absolute stillness existing in the unchanging law which itself arises in the divine consciousness and is inseparable from it. Of this Hermes writes, 'such then is the nature of this being: imperceptible, unlimited, unthinkable, immeasurable'.[9]

The Hermetic view of Man

However, the main focus of the *Asclepius* is Man. Hermes describes him as the second image of the Supreme, and the third god. Although as a class Man is placed below the daemons (spirits), through the power of association he has the potential to become whatever he associates with: any entity from God to matter. A man becomes similar to those with whom he lives.

Divine consciousness reaches down to human beings and is accessible to them through the power of attention. Before he begins an exposition of the threefold deity and the nature of Man, Hermes asks Asclepius to listen 'not only with keen attention, but with liveliness of mind'.[10] Before describing to his disciples how everything in the cosmos is interconnected, he warns, 'If you do not hear the words of the speaker with attentive obedience the discourse will fly over you and flow round you, or rather, it will flow back and mingle again with the waters of its own source.'[11] As always, it is the state of the student which determines the power of the master.

Access to divine consciousness gives human beings enormous power. Early in the work Hermes bursts into praise of Man, for Hermes has discovered Man's potential in himself. 'Man is a great miracle, a being to be adored and honoured. He passes into the nature of God as though he were God ....'[12] Praise in Hermes is a key element in transformation, a transformation which the discourse is intended to bring about.

Man has been made partly of divine substance and partly of matter. The true man 'views with contempt that part of nature in himself which is human since he has put his entire trust in the divinity of the other part.'[13] Unchanging spirit is the only ultimate reality for Hermes. It is the divine part of human beings that enables those who have found access to it to fulfil the first role for which Man was brought forth: to contemplate and reverence God. A god without worship is a god without power. St Matthew tells us (13, 56) that even Jesus could not do many mighty works in his own country because the people lacked faith in him.

Man's second role, not in reality different from the first, is to care for creation. He loves the creation just as he is beloved by the gods. Hermes emphasises Man's duty to the planet with a force of which there is a strong resonance today. He makes the point that to fulfil this obligation Man needs the physical body which he has been given. The body does not therefore imprison the human being, as in Plato, but rather exalts him. He has been placed according to Hermes in 'the fortunate middle position', a position which makes Man superior to the gods. But the position brings a danger. Because of their double nature human beings can identify with the divine, but equally through their physical body they can associate with matter and therefore sink to lower forms. They have free choice, which is the essence of their stature. They are bound to the consequences of that choice by the unchanging law. If 'we have completed our term of service, discharged our worldly duties and have been freed from the bonds of mortality, God (will) restore us to our higher, that is divine nature, free from blemish and inviolable'.[14] As in Plato the divine part of the soul is immortal.

Why should we make any other choice? This question seems to be in Asclepius' mind when he asks, 'Why has God permitted evil to be brought into the world?' Hermes explains that it is because 'the imperfections of matter' are 'mixed within bodies, together with other imperfections derived from the food and nourishment which we take through necessity, as do all living beings. It is therefore inevitable that the desires arising from greed and other vices of the mind steal into human souls.'[15] This greed takes the form of desire for possessions. These are alien to the parts of Man which have kinship with the divine. 'Thus we must despise not only those things we grasp at, but also the very source within us from which the grasping comes.'[16] The grasping comes from a man's corporeal nature which is nevertheless essential to his function in the cosmos. But if he seizes parts of the creation for himself he begins to associate with his corporeal nature and to forget the divine. As in Plato's *Phaedrus* (248) the soul which is unable to follow the gods 'sinks beneath the double load of forgetfulness and vice'.

It would require a major change in the emotional state of the disciple to reverse this process, but this is, perhaps, what is about to happen. God, says Hermes, gave us the best defence against the insidious enemy, 'When he deigned to bestow on the minds of men consciousness, knowledge and intelligence ... by these alone we can avoid the deceits of evil, trickery and vice.'[17] However, if we use these gifts selfishly, we suffer the consequence.

There is a day of judgement, as in Plato (*Republic* 10, 614). Hermes writes, 'When the soul has departed from the body it will come under the power of a most potent spirit who will examine its merits and judge it. When that spirit has discerned that the soul is pious and just, he permits it to remain in the region which it merits. But if he sees it covered with the stains of crime and oblivious of its vices he hurls it from the heights to the depths, delivering it to storms and whirlwinds, to the ever contending elements of air, fire and water so that it is caught between heaven and earth, continually buffeted in different directions by the turbulence of the world.'[18] If humans do not choose to come under the finer laws voluntarily, they come under the laws pertaining to matter which are governed by the three ineluctable forces of destiny, necessity and order. Immortality, says Hermes, then becomes a burden. The oldest recorded version of the Day of Judgement is an illustrated 'Spell' (125) in the Egyptian *Book of the Dead* (*c.* fourteenth century BC). It is curiously appropriate as it is Thoth who seems to be officiating and recording the result of the heart being weighed against the feather of truth (Fig. 1).

What is deplorable for Hermes is that education, instead of freeing the mind, helps to enthral it. Philosophy, he says, has become mingled with other subjects, for instance music, arithmetic and geometry, which has made it difficult to understand. Pure philosophy should attend to these other subjects just sufficiently to marvel at the knowledge that the heavenly bodies return regularly to the same predetermined positions, and to 'revere and praise the divine artistry and intelligence'. In Hermetic writing praise can lead directly to second birth. The proper study of music can reveal the One through the many. 'To understand music is to comprehend the arrangement of all things which is determined by divine proportion. By this proportion which comes from the supreme artist the arrangement of all individual things is transmuted into one.'[19]

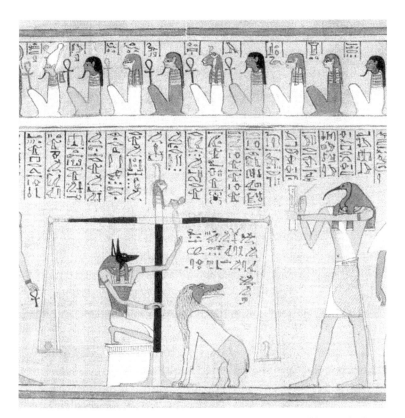

Figure 1. Spell 125 from the Book of the Dead. Ani and his wife Tutu watch as his heart is weighed against a feather representing Maat. Anubis checks the accuracy of the balance. Thoth (Hermes) stands ready to write down the result and the monster Ammit waits to gobble up any heart weighed down by sin.

The cycles of time

There was a strong awareness in ancient Egypt of the cyclical nature of time, an idea that is also present in Hesiod, Plato and Synesius. It is well reflected in the *Asclepius*. Each cycle started with a creative impulse which needed to be renewed, and

19

human participation was part of this cosmic event. The daily temple rituals accompanied the sun's rising and journey across the sky with all its perils, and worked to ensure that this was successfully accomplished. The New Year festival brought in the inundation on which the whole population depended. There were longer cycles too. The timing of all these festivals had deep significance for the re-alignment of society to Maat (the concept of justice and order).[20]

Hermes' prophecy

There is a prophecy in the *Aesclepius* which suggests that over a long cycle the departure from Maat had been very extensive. The memory of the function of Man had been lost. This had a grave effect not only on mankind but on nature.

> The gods will withdraw from earth to heaven .... Foreigners pouring into the land will neglect religion .... Duties to the gods and divine worship will be prohibited with penalties .... This holy land will be filled with sepulchres and the dead ... only stories of your religion will survive, and these your children will not believe .... Egypt will become a desert ... an example of the most ferocious cruelty ... the fruits of the earth will wither and the land will no longer be fertile. The very air will hang heavy in lifeless torpor .... Such will be the old age of the world: irreligion, disorder and unreason concerning all that is good.[21]

To understand the gravity of this one needs to consider further the Hermetic vision of the cosmos. It was based on a system of reflections. As has been said in the *Emerald Tablet*, attributed to Hermes, it is written, 'As above, so below.' The cosmos is the visible image of the Supreme. Man, also an image of the Supreme, has the function to reverence and care for the creation. Egypt had a special place within it. It was the 'the image of heaven', 'the temple of the whole cosmos'. It was particularly shocking that the inhabitants of this favoured land should forget their sacred trust.

There had been, perhaps, another insidious departure from Maat. This is described by Hermes as the creation of 'terrestrial gods'. He writes, 'Because our sceptical ancestors erred greatly in their opinion of the gods and gave no attention to worship and divine religion, they invented an art by which they could create gods.' The essence of this art was to make statues which were then enlivened by persuading spirits to dwell therein by sacred and divine rites. The statues could do harm, but also bring great benefits to men. 'These gods of ours help us as though they were loving parents: either they attend to particular matters, or they foretell the future through lot and divination, or they provide certain things, and by these means they come to help human beings, each in his own way.'[22] These terrestrial gods could also be regarded as a further example of the reflection of heaven on earth.

Why then does Hermes say, 'our sceptical ancestors erred greatly'? This seeming contradiction is not easy to resolve. But it does seem that the practice of enlivening statues is associated with 'giving no attention to worship and divine religion': in other words, neglecting the primary role of mankind. The benefits conferred by the terrestrial gods do not directly assist this function. The ancestors of Hermes and his disciples had apparently devised a method of obtaining the blessings of terrestrial gods, while not attending to their own responsibilities by ignoring the worship of the heavenly gods. In a way they had become prisoners of their own creation. These terrestrial gods could become angry and might need to be propitiated.

Hermes' prophecy is indeed dire, and yet is unusually accurate in specific detail. One may be filled with awe when one considers the fate of Egypt and the Egyptians, and compares it with the rich legacy of Greece and Rome which the West has inherited. The very race has disappeared. We see every day Celtic, Roman and Saxon types, but in Egypt one looks in vain for that reddish skin, the heads elongated to the rear, the almond eyes and full lips (see Fig. 2). Indeed the true successors to the Ancient Egyptians are to be found amongst those who have a strong affinity with their spirit.

It was not until the early nineteenth century that Egyptian hieroglyphics could be deciphered, and then only because of the discovery of the Rosetta Stone.[23] Many explanations are given of Egyptian architecture and yet the purpose and significance of the three great pyramids of Giza remain a mystery. Were they tombs? But there are no sarcophagi or original inscriptions. Egyptological tradition tells us that the Egyptians were a people obsessed with death and that this is the subject of their art. Yet more recent views explain that their theme was primarily life.[24] A great religion has been reduced to a series of children's stories. All this marks the oblivion of race, language and culture.

But when did this happen? Most scholars agree that the *Corpus Hermeticum* and *Asclepius* were composed between 100 and 300 AD. However, nothing of such a cataclysmic nature had happened to Egypt or even threatened to happen by the end of

Figure 2. Prince Khaemweset, son of Rameses III, depicted in his tomb in the Valley of the Queens.

the third century. Although there were many ancient predictions of coming disasters, this one seems surprisingly accurate in detail.

However, from these scenes of death and destruction springs renewal; the perfect order of Maat will be restored. 'Then the lord and father who is first in power and governor under God who is the One, will consider the conduct and wilful deeds of men ... he will take a stand against these evils .... Either he will dissolve all this in a flood, or consume it by fire .... Finally, he will restore the world to its ancient beauty. By these events the world will be reborn.'[25]

What was such a time like? The tradition is recorded in Manetho that for many years the country was ruled by heavenly gods.[26] In later times the pharaohs were presented as gods who had taken human form. But such divine men were not restricted to a pharaonic role. Men walked the earth who had become gods not by the report of others but by their own study and discipline. A man of such stature, who had wholly identified with the god Thoth, may have been the reputed author of the *Asclepius* which, unlike the *Corpus Hermeticum*, reads as though written by a single person.

Hermes

Hermes was the title that the ancient Greeks gave to the Egyptian god Thoth, for the attributes assigned to Thoth by the Egyptians seemed to be similar to those assigned to Hermes by the Greeks (and to Mercury by the Romans).

His symbol in Egypt was the ibis, a bird which was found in large numbers on the Nile in ancient times. The ibis was a fitting bird to represent Hermes, since it has a long pointed beak, appropriate for the god who invented writing and letters. According to Plato, when Theuth (Thoth) offered the gift of reading and writing to King Thamus (Ammon), the King was displeased because he said it would weaken the memory of his subjects.[27] Thoth and Hermes were also associated with number and counting, and they carried messages and prayers to the gods and guidance from the gods to men. The Egyptian god Thoth (though not the Greek Hermes) was also considered to have been the voice of Ra (the Supreme) and to have spoken the creation into existence. A man who had fully realised the qualities of Thoth in himself was thus well qualified to discourse on the nature of God, the Cosmos and Man.

Hermes Trismegistus

The first mention of Hermes with the triple appellation of great ('greatest and greatest and great') is in a record of a meeting of the council of the ibis cult in Hermopolis in 172 BC.[28] Cicero, Ovid and Apuleius knew of him. The latter was formerly credited with the translation of the Greek text of *Asclepius* into Latin.

Writing to Porphyry in the third century AD, the Neoplatonist Iamblichus showed great respect to Hermes. Under the assumed Egyptian name of Abamon, Iamblichus writes: 'It is to him that our ancestors in particular dedicated the fruits of their wisdom, attributing all their own writing to Hermes. And if we, for our part, receive from this god our due share of favour you, for your part, do well in laying before the priests questions about theology.' Emma Clarke explains: 'The exact identity of Hermes named here is deliberately ambiguous. "Abamon" exploits the supposed attribute of both the Greek Hermes and the (semi-)divine Hermes Trismegistus, a late antique amalgam of Thoth and Hermes.'[29]

Hermetics and Gnostics

Christianity in the first and second centuries AD was permeated by the views of the Gnostic sects, for these sects found it easy to convert to Christianity. The Gnostics, like the Hermetic cult, arose in Egypt, although there was also a rather different form of Gnosticism which spread from Persia and Syria. There are some striking similarities between Gnostic and Hermetic beliefs. The Gnostics derived their name from their view of knowledge. This was not something that was to be learnt from a book, or heard from another person, but it was received through 'gnosis':[30] an inward experience of revelation, a sudden illumination. The effect was not dissimilar from that described by Hermes on p. 13. It is also significant that the examples of second birth given in the *Corpus Hermeticum* accord in spirit with gnosis. One example is the description in *Corpus,*13, 'O father, I have been made steadfast through God; I see not with the eyes, but by the operation of spiritual energy in the powers. I am in heaven, in earth, in water, in air; I am in living creatures and in plants; I am in the womb, before the womb, after the womb. I am present everywhere.' There are Gnostic texts which express a very similar enlightenment, for instance the anonymous author of *The Thunder: Perfect Mind* writes 'I am the first and the last. I am the honoured one and the scorned one. I am the whore and the holy one. I am the wife and the virgin.'[31]

Apart from the similarity between the concept of gnosis and that of 'second birth', as used in the *Corpus*, there is a similarity in the way concepts, even Platonic ones, are expressed and a similarity in the use of idiom and figure. For instance, the word *pleroma* has a special significance, both in the Gnostic writings and in the Hermetic. The classical meanings of the word centre round 'completeness' and 'fullness'. St Paul extends the definition of the word to describe the full and perfect nature.[32] But to the Gnostics it conveyed the sense of the 'abode of the Almighty'. The word is used in this sense in *Corpus Hermeticum,*16,3, where Hermes describes the *pleroma* as being the One and in the One.

Aion is another word which carried a meaning peculiar to Hermetists and Gnostics alike. In Classical Greek it meant 'a long time', 'everlasting time', 'eternity'. In Hermetic and Gnostic writing it also meant 'absolute', the 'supreme deity'.

The word 'drunkenness' acquired the non-classical meaning of being so immersed in worldly affairs that the words of Truth cannot be heard. Jesus says in the Gnostic *Gospel of Thomas*, 'I found them all drunk; I found none of them athirst.'[33] Hermes enquires, 'Whither are you being carried, O men, drunk as you are, having swallowed neat the word of ignorance?'[34]

If there was a mingling of the two traditions it seems more likely that the Hermetic writings influenced the Gnostic than vice versa, since there seems to be hardly any awareness of Christianity in the Hermetic writing. This is true even in the prophecy of Egypt's destruction, which might have allowed an opportunity for it without disturbing the ancient Egyptian setting. On the other hand the Gnostic Christians do seem to have used Hermetic texts for devotional purposes. This is emphasised by their inclusion in the Nag Hammadi Library. The great majority of these texts are written in Coptic from a Judaeo-Christian standpoint. The inclusion of four Hermetic works in a collection of Gnostic devotional literature is an indication that Hermetic literature was considered an integral part of Gnostic study or devotion. This view is reinforced by the fact that one of these pieces is a note from the scribe to the recipient saying that he has many more Hermetic texts but has not included them because he believed that his recipient already had them.[35] The circulation of

Hermetic texts amongst the early Christians may well have been much greater than has been generally recognised.

In considering the question of Hermetic influence on Gnosticism, attention should be given to the dating of texts. The approximate dates usually accepted for the composition of the philosophic Hermetica are 100-300 AD. It is also thought that the Greek original of the *Asclepius* was written towards the end of that period, although the grounds for this are by no means firm. Copenhaver indicates evidence from the texts that Hermetic collections of some kind circulated as early as the second or third centuries. J.P. Mahé points out that the material on which individual treatises are based may come from the first century AD or even earlier.[36] Clement of Alexandria, writing in the first half of the third century, claims knowledge of 42 Hermetic books (*Stromata* 1, 15). Bearing in mind the extreme difficulty of establishing dates for these works, chronology alone does not rule out Hermetic influence on the Gnostics during the first two centuries of the Christian era.

The nature of the Hermetic texts is also significant. One of these is the *Discourse on the Eighth and Ninth (Spheres)* which contains a passage describing gnosis or second birth. This gnosis, as is usual in the Hermetica, is accompanied by a hymn of praise. The discourse is followed by another piece which consists of a hymn of praise probably connected to the *Discourse*.[37] It contains these words, 'We rejoice because while we were in the body you made us divine through your knowledge.' In other words, these two texts contain the essence of both Gnosticism and Hermeticism: union with the Supreme while still in the body, an event which was characteristically accompanied by praise.

Although the Gnostic sects held widely different views from each other, there was nevertheless a core of beliefs which was common to most, and much of this core, shorn of its Christian clothing, is found in the Hermetica. The essential gnosis was the oneness of the Supreme. This signified more than what is generally meant by monotheism in the Judaic or Christian traditions. God in his aspect of Father did not make the cosmos. He *is* the cosmos and there is nothing else. This statement of absolute unity is made at the opening of the *Asclepius* and also in Gnostic literature. Jesus says in the *Gospel of Thomas* (the best known of the Nag Hammadi texts), 'When you make the two one, and you make the inner as the outer and the outer as the inner, so that you will make the male and the female into a single one .... Then shall you enter the Kingdom.'[38] Here Jesus is not just proclaiming a fact; he is pointing to a profound spiritual realisation to be attained through gnosis.

What then of the apparent plurality? As you approach it, it is seen not to exist. 'Where you see birth there you see delusion,' says Hermes.[39] The Nag Hammadi *Treatise on the Resurrection* says of the Resurrection: 'it is no illusion, but it is truth! Indeed it is more fitting to say that the world is an illusion.' Hermetists, like the Gnostics, considered only spirit to be real.

The references to making the male and the female one in the *Gospel of Thomas* are particularly significant because there is distinctive emphasis in the Gnostic tradition on the importance of women. The sense that each sex contained the powers of the other goes back to Ancient Egypt (see Fig. 3). Hermes has an allegorical passage on how men and women exchange qualities in the sexual act, and it is particularly pointed out in the *Corpus* that Man in truth is beyond gender.[40]

29

Figure 3. Statue from Karnac of the pharaoh Akhenaten, who considered himself the embodiment of the supreme deity. He is portrayed with both male and female characteristics.

The human being who has understood that both genders are within, has realised the common archetype to them both. 'I am the Father, I am the mother, I am the son,' exclaims a divine being in the *Apocryphon of John*.[41] Such beings contain the creation within them. They are the All. In the *Gospel of Thomas* Jesus says, 'But the kingdom is in your centre and it is about you.'[42] Hermes has come to the same realisation when he declares, 'But you are whatsoever I am; you are whatever I do; you are whatever I speak. You are all things and there is nothing else.'[43] How then does apparent evil enter the world and what is its cause? The root cause is ignorance. It is the ignorance leading to desire for possessions that has to be removed. As has already been mentioned, God has equipped men with consciousness, knowledge and intelligence for this purpose.[44]

In the *Corpus* Hermes gives an allegorical account of Man wishing to create and receiving the assent, though not the command, of the Supreme. He does create; but seeing his reflection in Nature, mistakes it for himself and uniting with Nature in love falls into all manner of suffering. In *Poimandres* (the title of the first book in the *Corpus*) the Nous of the supreme rescues the soul from such ignorance.

The accounts of the origin of evil by the Gnostic leaders Basilides and Valentinus are quite similar in imagery. The man becomes possessed by evil entities, but it is he himself who has led his desire towards evil. Like Hermes, Valentinus supposes that the lower soul, without the will of her father and without having realised her divine nature, plunged into forbidden territory in order to know her father. She is rescued by the saviour who healed her passions and separated them from her by bestowing gnosis.[45] The inner meaning of these myths is the same: gnosis of the nature of one's real self is the only antidote to evil.

It must have been plain to Gnostics and Hermetists alike that most human beings do not fulfil their potential in this life. It must also have been clear that while some humans appear to make little spiritual progress during their life upon earth, others make much progress very quickly. To the Gnostics and Hermetists the presumption was that such souls had been previously embodied, and during that embodiment spiritual development had taken place. The fact that some babies were born deformed led some to think they were suffering the consequences of injustices that they had committed in a previous life-time (the voicing of which opinion once cost an England football manager his job).

From the beginning of the second century AD Gnosticism came under the attack of the Orthodox Church. Perhaps this was partly because the orthodox party felt that, under the threat of persecution, a tighter organisation and definition of fundamental Christian beliefs needed to be made. The Church also felt the need for a single literal text that everyone, even the uneducated, could understand. The fear was that several levels of meaning in the Scriptures would lead to confusion and to individuals interpreting them in their own ways. But the Gnostics, like the Hermetists, much favoured allegory, and they began to feel themselves excluded from the orthodox body of the Church. Allegorical interpretation of the scriptures did not die even in the Orthodox Church. St Augustine in particular commends it. With approval he quotes St Ambrose as saying, 'the letter killeth but the spirit quickeneth'. He goes on to explain how if certain passages were taken literally they might lead a man to 'perverse belief', but when spiritually opened by Ambrose the 'mystical veil' for him had been removed from such texts.[46] Probably later, he insists (unlike some Gnostic writers) that everything written in the scriptures must be literally true. But he writes of certain passages, 'I view them with greater delight under that (figurative) aspect than if no such figure were drawn from the sacred books, though the fact would remain the same and the knowledge the same.'[47] The allegorical interpretation of the Scriptures also persisted in the Desert fathers and eventually in the monastic tradition, which later sprang from that earlier one. This method of interpreting the Scriptures eventually gave birth to the fourfold sense fully adopted in the Middle Ages, and formulated in particular by St Thomas Aquinas.[48]

'Hermes' in the Asclepius seems to foreshadow different levels of comprehending truth when he writes of intelligence and consciousness. 'Now the intelligence of human consciousness ... consists totally in the memory of past events .... But the intelligence of Nature can be attained through the capacity of cosmic consciousness from everything which is subject to the senses in the world. The consciousness of Eternity, which comes next, has also been bestowed and its quality made known by the sensory world. But the intelligence and quality of the consciousness belonging to the Supreme God is truth alone.'[49]

The four senses of which St Thomas Aquinas speaks are literal or historic, allegorical, tropological (moral), and anagogical. He says of the last: insofar as things 'signify what is involved in eternal glory, we have the anagogical sense'. This seems to come close to Hermes' description of 'the consciousness belonging to the Supreme God': truth alone. There is also a connection between the literal or historic level and Hermes' view that 'the intelligence of human consciousness is totally in the memory of past events'.

Nevertheless, despite the continuance of this tradition in the Orthodox Church, at least from the early years of the second century the Church claimed to be the sole mediator of the meaning of scripture and even of Christ. This claim eliminated all direct mystical experience of truth. Thus there was a conflict between 'membership' of the Church and direct knowledge or gnosis.[50]

The orthodox party based its position on four bulwarks: acceptance of the authority of only those books which became canonical; acceptance of the authority of the Old Testament; total obedience to the bishop; belief in a literal interpretation of the New Testament. By the end of the second century Gnostics had been virtually expelled from the Church.

In the tradition of the early Church, deep religious experience arises from within and constitutes the real spiritual life. Obedience to laws, bishops, and councils, and verbal declarations of belief might or might not assist that life, but they could never be a substitute for it. Gnosis was the true knowledge; the rest was just information, right or wrong.

A light went out of the Church with the departure of the Gnostics, and with the take-over by Constantine and his successors the darkness deepened. But the fire of the spirit can never be extinguished and the centre of spiritual practice, the essence of Gnosticism, retreated to the monasteries and hermitages of Egypt, and later of Europe.

The influence of Hermes lived on. Two Church Fathers had a good deal to say about him but held very different views. St

Augustine tells us that Hermes lived in the time of Moses and was responsible for writing the *Asclepius*.[51] However, Augustine condemned him as an idolator. Lactantius saw him as an inspired seer who, long before the Christian era, had correctly written about the one God, the Word and the creation. These two opposing views were taken up by later writers in the Middle Ages. It was that of Lactantius which prevailed.

Hermes in the Middle East and Spain

The Hermetic works aroused considerable interest among the Arabic scholars in the early Middle Ages, an account of which is contained in Brian Copenhaver's introduction to his *Hermetica* (xlv-xlvii) and also in Walter Scott's *Hermetica* (1,97-111). According to Scott, Hermeticism together with Greek paganism (albeit modified by Syriac and Mithraic influences) survived in Harran, a city of Northern Mesopotamia. In order to be accepted by the Muslim authorities the inhabitants took the name of Sabian, the name of one of the books whose followers were exempted from persecution by the Koran.

Harran produced a number of scholars. The greatest was Thabit ibn Qurrah, who was much influenced by Neoplatonism as well as by the Hermetica. Scott considered it possible that when growing persecution extinguished 'Harranianism' in its original city (*c.* 1050) some of its followers might have rekindled Hermeticism in Byzantium during the eleventh century, in the time of the scholar Psellus. If this were true, and it is only a surmise, it would be an example of Arabic scholars rekindling knowledge and enthusiasm among Westerners for their own tradition.

There is a clearer example of Arabic culture assimilating Hermetic ideas which later returned to the West and kindled new interest there. Toledo was a focal point in Europe for the translation of works from Arabic into Latin and vernacular languages. These were undertaken in the reign of Alphonso X, King of Castile (1252-1284), known as The Wise, who commissioned the translation of a great many works, collected into three large miscellanies. These covered respectively magic, astronomy and astrology. Evelyn Procter says of the first of these, 'No date is given and the King is not mentioned, but the manuscript has all the characteristics of a royal manuscript, and the contents appear to correspond to part of the Latin *Liber Picatrix*, which has survived in manuscripts of the fifteenth century and later, and which is stated to be based on a vernacular translation made at Alfonso's command in 1256.'[52] According to Frances Yates, 'Though the authorship of *Picatrix* is not assigned to Hermes Trismegistus, the work mentions him with great respect, and it is important because it may have been one of Ficino's authorities on talismans and sympathetic magic.'[53]

Although the *Picatrix* is primarily a book on magic, it has a philosophical setting which is both Hermetic and Ficinian. The *Picatrix*, like the *Asclepius,* begins with intimations that profound secrets are to be revealed. The truth is One: 'all things come from it, and through it receive truth and unity in the perpetual movement of generation and corruption. There is a hierarchy in things, and lower things are raised to higher things. Man is a little world reflecting the great world of the Cosmos, but through his intellect the wise man can raise himself above the seven heavens.'[54] Through the medium of astrology and theurgy in the *Picatrix* many would have learnt the principles of Plato and Hermes. Perhaps the true magic of Trismegistus was to combine these subjects with philosophy (a practice he condemns).

Hermes in the Middle Ages: France, Germany and Italy

It may seem strange to introduce an account of Hermes in the Middle Ages with Dionysius (known as pseudo-Dionysius) since he was an anonymous monk born in the sixth century, who wrote his work under the name of Dionysius the Areopagite, the Greek who was converted by St Paul during his visit to Athens.[55] Yet because of the intensity of his writing and the fact that until the late Renaissance his work was believed to have been that of the Areopagite, he was responsible for bringing into Christianity ideas emanating from Plato and Hermes.

He takes up Hermes' proposition that 'either all things are of one, or they are one'. Therefore, like Hermes, he maintains that either God should have all names or no name. But he develops this statement into spiritual practices. The first of these is the Way of Affirmation. The second is the Way of Negation.[56] But they are to be pursued differently: 'When we made assertions we began with the first things, moved down through intermediate terms, until we reached the last things. But now as we climb from the last things up to the most primary we deny all things.' The second exercise succeeds the first. What do we experience on this journey? 'The more we take flight upward, the more our words are confined to the ideas we are capable of forming: so that now as we plunge into that darkness which is beyond intellect, we shall find ourselves not simply running short of words but actually speechless and unknowing.'[57]

These words might have been taken from *The Cloud of Unknowing,* composed many centuries later. Like Hermes, Dionysius describes the cosmos as governed by a hierarchy, but Dionysius is more orderly and precise in his enumeration and description of the heavenly host. It is grouped into three orders of three: Seraphim (burns what separates man from God), Cherubim (fullness of knowledge), Thrones (established in divine service); Dominions (order and justice), Virtues (bestow grace and valour), Powers (overcome fetters to the earth); Principalities (Divine Lordship and service), Archangels (imprint on everything the divine seal and impart to the soul spiritual light), Angels (minister to all men and Nature, purifying and uplifting them).

Through the ministry of these orders the divine life is transmitted from its ultimate source to all things. These orders thus have an inner relationship with every human soul. Through them it may become liberated from material bondage and attain to the fullness of divine likeness.[58] The divine ray constantly flows into us, yet it can never be deprived of its unity. Dionysius' treatment thus illustrates Hermes' statement that 'Either all things are of one or they are one. The two propositions are so linked that it is impossible to separate one from the other.' It also shows, as in Hermes, how the creation is a great chain of being, sustained by love and perpetually renewed by the Absolute.

In *The Ecclesiastical Hierarchy* Dionysius again strongly echoes Hermes in maintaining that the order upon earth reflects the order above. For the three primary orders are reflected in the three ecclesiastical orders: bishops, priests and deacons.

In the twelfth-century Renaissance the reputation of Hermes was high, Abelard and Alain of Lille both thought Hermes a man of great wisdom, for his reputation as a magician did not damage his name as a philosopher. This was in spite of the fact that many magical texts attributed to Hermes had begun to appear. There were serious attacks upon him as an idolator in the early thirteenth century. But both Roger Bacon and Albert the Great praised him as a philosopher, in spite of the magical works attributed to him.[59]

Although Meister Eckhart (1260-1307) does not mention Hermes or his two philosophical works by name, he does mention a book attributed to him: *The Twenty-four Philosophers*.[60] Eckhart's biographer writes that 'his entrance into the Dominican Order guaranteed him an immensely privileged education and access to the finest libraries. There is little philosphical or theological material extant which we can assume Meister Eckhart did not read.'[61] In any event his views and inspiration are very similar to those of Hermes. The One, he says, is everywhere present since all exists only by reference to it. 'Those who are rightly disposed ... intend God alone, and all things become God for them.' God and the soul, in its essence, are one.

An interest in the Hermetic writings runs through all the works of Nicholas of Cusa from *Sermo* 1 (1430) to *De ludo globi* (1463): the knowledge of the divine Word, the doctrine of divine names, and the concept of matter, world and man are taken from the *Asclepius*. Illustrative of his interest are the numerous glosses in Nicholas' own hand, found in the margins of the most ancient manuscript of the *Asclepius*. While Nicholas has to condemn the Hermetic passages on enlivening statues in *De pace fidei* he absolves Hermes of any accusation of idolatory in *de docta ignorantia*.[62] On a voyage from Byzantium to Italy Nicholas of Cusa had the 'intuition of opposites'. God is above all opposites and unites in himself statements that are incompatible in the finite world. This Hermetic principle became the central theme of Cusa's thought. All affirmation about God, such as being and non-being, encompassing all beings, and being contained in all beings is merely partial. It has to be completed by the contrary affirmation, because God unites in Himself that which is incompatible in the finite. God is nowhere in the world, while being everywhere in it.[63] Hermes and Dionysius will be recognised at once in the formulation of this paradox.

The Renaissance

In Renaissance times the profundity of Hermes' philosophy made a strong appeal to Marsilio Ficino, the great Florentine philosopher who revived the teaching of Plato in the West as a direct source of spiritual illumination. He was able to do this by building on the information supplied by St Augustine in the City of God, an ironical circumstance since Augustine reserves for Hermes some of his most severe strictures.

Not only did Hermes live in the time of Moses, but he was the first in a chain of philosophers which was directly linked to Moses. Ficino bases this concept of a chain on Artapanus,[64] the second century BC Jewish writer. The chain that Ficino describes was a teacher/disciple relationship: it began with Hermes Trismegistus and was completed with Plato. The implication of this was that the teaching of Plato, and his school, was based upon Moses, just as was the authority of the Hebrew prophets through whose inspiration the coming of Christ was foretold. This made the stature of Hermes and his successors comparable to that of those prophets, well above anything that they had enjoyed even in the Middle Ages.

In 1462 Cosimo de' Medici, the effective ruler of Florence, set Marsilio up in a small villa, close to his own at Careggi, now a suburb of Florence. Ficino was given the task of producing a Latin translation of Plato's works, in which Cosimo was keenly interested. However, shortly after Ficino had settled to his task, one of Cosimo's agents had discovered in what is now Bulgaria the Greek text of the *Corpus Hermeticum*. Cosimo purchased the manuscript and had it conveyed to Careggi, where he instructed Ficino to desist from translating Plato, so beloved by the great ruler, and to translate Hermes first. Such was the veneration in which he held Hermes. Ficino's close connection with the *Asclepius* is perhaps suggested by the fact that a Latin version is erroneously included in his *Opera Omnia* printed in Basle in 1576. Pico della Mirandola's essay, 'On the Dignity of Man', may be inspired by the encomium in the *Asclepius*.

But Hermes' reputation was not confined to Florence. A remarkable tribute is the huge depiction of Hermes in mosaic on the pavement of Siena Cathedral (Fig. 4).

Almost as great a tribute to his sacred authority are the series of pictures which Pinturicchio was commissioned to paint of Hermes and which now decorate the inner papal apartments in the Vatican. One of these features the goddess Isis apparently instructing Moses on one side of her and Hermes on the other (Fig. 5).

41

Figure 4. *Hermes Trismegistus,* mosaic by Giovanni di Stefano, Siena Cathedral. Hermes appears to be instructing two Egyptians. Frances Yates (p. 116) suggests that one of them may be Moses. The title at the foot reads (translated), 'Hermes Trismegistus, contemporary of Moses'. The Latin quotation to the right is taken from Lactantius, who has adapted a passage from *Asclepius.*

In the second half of the sixteenth century scholars began to doubt the antiquity of the Hermetic texts and finally Isaac Casaubon, in 1614, convinced most scholars that the texts and content of the *Corpus* and *Asclepius* dated from the Christian era. This was still the view of Nock and Festugière, who pub-

Figure 5. *Isis with Hermes Trismegistus and Moses* by Pinturicchio, Room of the Saints, Borgia Apartments, Vatican. Isis is instructing Moses (right) and Hermes (left). See Frances Yates, pp. 115-16.

lished an excellent critical edition of the *Corpus* and *Asclepius* shortly after World War II.

Sources of the *Asclepius* and
Corpus Hermeticum

Scholars have found Stoic and Judaeic influences in the *Asclepius* and *Corpus Hermeticum*, but the genius of Plato shines through far more strongly. There is his vision of the ineffable One which though unmanifest to the senses, illumines the true forms of the virtues. They too then shine with the same light. What we see in the physical world are only shadows and images of these forms. Hermes says that no trace of the consciouness of God can be seen on earth.[65] Nevertheless, Man is a divine being and with philosophical training this intelligible light can be apprehended by the human mind. In Plato, as in Hermes, the One is generative. It begets from itself a creator god, the Cosmos, from which everything is born. This second god is the manifest image of the unmanifest.

Jeremy Naydler points out that the Platonic conception of the human soul is very different from the earlier Homeric conception where it is represented as a kind of wraith of the individual when alive. Plato's conception is much more akin to that of Pythagoras where the soul (*psuchê*) is the inner nature of the human being. Its essence is immortal and divine.[66] It is the ultimate destiny of this essence to unite with the unmanifest One. This view of the soul is also that of Hermes.

Whence did Plato derive his teaching? Every man in one sense is the source of his own knowledge; yet no one is independent of cultural tradition. Plato inherited many of the teachings of the Pythagoreans; and he had ample opportunity to become acquainted with them during his visits to Italy. But both Plato and Pythagoras had also visited Egypt and studied under Egyptian priests.[67]

The authority of the ancient biographers for the visits of Pythagoras and Plato to Egypt has been discounted by many modern scholars. It is sometimes explained that a visit to Egypt was a necessary element in the *curriculum vitae* of a philosopher if his credentials were to be taken seriously, and might therefore have been added as a polite fiction by an admiring biographer. If Egypt had had such a reputation it would only make it the more likely that aspiring philosophers or theologians would in fact have made this comparatively easy journey.

As Jeremy Naydler remarks, if Plato had visited Egypt he would have heard a similar teaching to that which he sets forth in his dialogues. He would have discovered the prototype of the Good, the Fair, the One, in Ra, the all-pervading and transcendent God. He would have discovered his *psuchê* in the Egyptian Ba, for it too had wings to fly to the Eternal; and the divine and immortal part of the soul he would have seen in the Egyptian *akh*.

Plato would also have witnessed, and perhaps taken part in, ceremonies intended to bring about spiritual rebirth in this life. The climax of the Sed festival, which theoretically celebrated thirty years of a king's reign, appears to have been connected with the reunion of the king with Ra. This festival was certainly being celebrated at the beginning of the Old Kingdom in the reign of Zoser (2668-2649 BC). The idea of union with Ra was still alive in the New Kingdom (1570-1070 BC) and a number of 'spells' in the Book of the Dead are witness to this. 'I am Ra who is with the gods and I will not perish' (Spell 8). The essence of these ceremonies was the total identification of the aspirant with the deity, such as is expressed in *Corpus Hermeticum* 5, 11: 'You are whatsoever I am, you are whatever I do; you are whatever I speak; you are all things and there is nothing else.'

The mystery of transformation into the divine after purificatory rites and ceremonies was inherited by the mystery cults of Greece, with which Plato was familiar (*Phaedrus* 250). The concept of transformation in the 'mysteries' was later adapted to the Eucharist of the Christian Church. That tradition is therefore still alive.

The essential ideas in Plato that have already been mentioned, as well as others, were reflected in the symbolism of Ancient Egypt. Many of these ideas we are more accustomed to associate with the East, and with India in particular. Some of them are in fact extraordinarily ancient and formative to our civilisation. We may respond to them more easily through our own tradition than when we receive them through a different culture. Nowhere do we hear these ideas more concisely or more powerfully than in the writings attributed to Hermes Trismegistus. Perhaps this is the true legacy of Ancient Egypt.

Conclusion

Although belief in the extreme antiquity of these texts had been demolished by Casaubon, they were still respected by some for the power of their content. These included Ralph Cudworth, the Cambridge Platonist, Thomas Taylor, the translator and commentator on the works of Plato, and Ralph Waldo Emerson, the foremost figure of the New England Transcendentalists, who wrote 'The high priesthood of pure reason, the Trismegisti' are 'expounders of the principles of thought from age to age. When we turn over their abstruse pages, wonderful seems the calm and grand air of these few, these great spiritual lords.' At such times, he writes, 'I am present at the sowing of the seed of the world'.[68]

The importance of Hermes Trismegistus is in the end less in the sources of his teaching than in the guidance he gives to everyone for the spiritual life. For such guidance does not change over the millennia. There are passages in Hermes which may be read in a few seconds and yet contemplated for a lifetime. The best way to evaluate Hermes is to reflect upon what he says.

Notes to the Introduction

Full publication details are provided in the Bibliography.

1. *Asclepius*, 1.
2. St Matthew 7:6.
3. *Asclepius*, 1.
4. Ibid., 3.
5. Ibid.
6. Ibid.
7. Ibid., 32.
8. Ibid., 31.
9. Ibid.; cf. *Corpus Hermeticum*, 13,6, and Plato, *Parmenides*, 137-42.
10. *Asclepius*, 10.
11. *Asclepius*, 19.
12. Ibid., 6; cf. *Corpus Hermeticum*, 5,11; 11,20.
13. Ibid.
14. Ibid., 11; cf. Plato, *Republic*, X, 614-21.
15. *Asclepius*, 22.
16. Ibid., 11.
17. Ibid., 16.
18. Ibid., 28.
19. *Asclepius,* 13; cf. Plato, *Timaeus,* 34-6. The proportions of established musical scales express this reminder of unity. The exemplar of these scales is described by Plato when he discusses the formation of the world soul.

The subjects touched upon in this paragraph – geometry, arithmetic, music and astronomy – were central to the curriculum of Plato's Academy and became known as the Quadrivium in the Middle Ages.

Together with the Trivium it formed the basis of Western education in the Middle Ages and beyond.

20. Jeremy Naydler, *Temple of the Cosmos,* pp. 91-3 and 147-52. As well as discussing the celebration of First Time, Naydler also writes about its reality being beyond the dimension of ordinary time.

21. *Asclepius,* 24-6.

22. Ibid., 37-8.

23. The Rosetta stone commemorates the benefactions conferred by Ptolemy V (205-180 BC) in three writing systems: hieroglyphics, demotic and Greek. The inscription is in two languages: Egyptian and Greek.

24. Jeremy Naydler, *Shamanic Wisdom in the Pyramid Texts,* passim.

25. *Asclepius,* 26.

26. Manetho, *History of Egypt,* 1,1.

27. Plato, *Phaedrus,* 274.

28. Brian P. Copenhaver, *Hermetica,* pp. xiv-xv.

29. Iamblichus, *De mysteriis,* 1,1, tr. Clarke, Dillon and Hershbelt.

30. *Gnôsis,* Greek for knowledge, wisdom.

31. *Nag Hammadi Library,* ed. J.M. Robinson, p. 297.

32. Romans 11:12.

33. Hugh McGregor Ross, *Gospel of Thomas,* 28.

34. *Corpus Hermeticum,* 7,1.

35. *Nag Hammadi Library,* pp. 321-8.

36. J.P. Mahé, quoted by Copenhaver, xliv.

37. *Nag Hammadi Library,* p.329.

38. Ross, *Gospel of Thomas,* 22.

39. *Asclepius,* 32.

40. *Corpus Hermeticum,* 1,15.

41. *Nag Hammadi Library,* p. 105.

42. Ross, *Gospel of Thomas,* 3.

43. *Corpus Hermeticum,* 5, 11.

44. *Asclepius,* 16.

45. Valentinus, Letter quoted in Joseph P. Macchio, *Orthodox Suppression of Original Christianity,* p. 164.
http://web.archive.org/web/20041010000727/www.essene.com/Church/Conspiracy/

46. St Augustine, *Confessions,* 6,4.

47. St Augustine, *On Christian Doctrine*, II, 6,7-8.

48. St Thomas Aquinas, *Summa Theologia,* 1,9-10. Also see Angela Voss, 'From Allegory to Anagoge: The Question of Symbolic Perception in a Literal World', www.skyscript.co.uk/allegory.html.

49. *Asclepius,* 32

50. For this information I am indebted to Dr Joseph Milne.

51. St Augustine, *City of God,* 8,23 and 18, 8.

52. Evelyn Procter, *Alfonso X of Castile,* 2, p. 10.

53. Frances Yates, *Giordano Bruno and the Hermetic Tradition,* 3, p. 49.

54. Ibid., 3, p. 51.

55. Acts 17:34.

56. Dionysius, *Mystical Theology,* 2-3.

57. Ibid.

58. Dionysius, *Celestial Hierarchy,* 3,2.

59. For the account of Hermes' reputation in the Middle Ages I am much indebted to Paolo Lucentini's excellent article 'Hermes Trismegistus, II: Middle Ages', in the *Dictionary of Gnosis and Western Esotericism.*

60. For this information I am indebted to Dr Joseph Milne.

61. Meister Eckhart's *Selected Writings*, tr. Oliver Davies, p. xviii.

62. Lucentini, op. cit.

63. J.M. Counet, 'Nicholas of Cusa', *Dictionary of Gnosis and Western Esotericism.*

64. See Yates, op. cit., 2, p. 26.

65. *Aesclepius,* 32.

66. Jeremy Naydler, *Plato, Shamanism and Ancient Egypt,* pp. 22-5

67. Clement of Alexandria, *Stromata,* 1,15. Clement says that Pythagoras was a disciple of Sonches the Egyptian archprophet and Plato of Sechnuphis of Heliopolis. Iamblichus and Porphyry also vouch for Pythagoras' visit to Egypt and Diogenes Laertius for that of Plato. Herodotus (book 2) writes that 'the names of nearly all the gods came to Greece from Egypt'. In the *Timaeus* Plato makes an Egyptian priest say to Solon, 'O Solon, Solon, you Greeks are all children!' (*Timaeus* 22). Egypt was the repository of ancient knowledge.

68. Ralph Waldo Emerson, *Selected Writings of Ralph Waldo Emerson*, p. 303.

Translator's Note

For the text of the Latin the critical edition of D. Nock and A-J. Festugière has been followed (Les Belles Lettres, Paris, 1992 [1st edn 1946]). Reference has also been made to the most important of the early manuscripts, Bruxellensis 10054-10056 (early eleventh century).

The division of the text into numbered sections, although not in the manuscript, has become conventional in printed editions. These divisions have been indicated in the translation that follows by bold numbers in square brackets. I have added headings to indicate the main subject of the section.

Some words are difficult to translate, especially where the Latin word has no exact English equivalent. *Mundus*, for instance, has generally been translated as 'cosmos', but this does not always convey the best sense. It has sometimes therefore been translated differently. Where this is so, *mundus* has been added after the translation in square brackets. In the *Asclepius*, *mundus* can also mean 'matter'.

Similarly, *species* has a much broader meaning in Latin that the nearest equivalent word in English. It has been mostly translated as 'form', 'individual form' or 'individual' as seems in each case to make the best sense.

Genus has also been difficult to translate. In the *Asclepius* it conveys something more than simply 'race', 'kind' or 'class'. It is associated with generative power and is referred to as 'immortal'. There is resonance here with the Platonic 'idea'. The English word often used in this translation is 'archetype', meaning the original pattern from which all copies are produced, though on some occasions the word 'class' has seemed preferable.

The nearest equivalent in English to the Latin *daimon* (or *daemon*) is 'spirit', but this has such a variety of meaning that in most cases it has been felt better to use 'daemon'. Occasionally 'spirit' has been used where there seems no danger of confusion.

Translation

Teacher and disciples

[1] 'It is God, yes, God, who has led you to me, O Asclepius, so that you can take part in a divine discourse. This discourse will be such that through its love and reverence for God it will rightly seem to have more divine power than any I have previously spoken, or rather than any that have been inspired in me by the divine spirit. If you show yourself able to understand it your whole mind will be completely filled with all that is good, that is if there are many good things and not one only in which all are held. Indeed, one can see that these alternatives are consistent with each other; either all things are of one, or they are one. The two propositions are so linked that it is impossible to separate one from the other. But this you will find out if you attend carefully to the coming discourse. But now, Asclepius, you must move forward a little. Call Tat to come and join us.'

At Tat's entry Asclepius suggested that Hammon also be present. Trismegistus said, 'No ill-will prevents Hammon from joining us, for I well remember that many of my writings have been dedicated to him, just as many discourses on natural philosophy and countless public discourses have been dedicated to my most loving and beloved son Tat. But on this treatise I shall inscribe your name. Call no one except Hammon lest a conversation worthy of such reverence and on such a profound subject be profaned by the arrival and presence of many people. For it is the mark of an irreligious mind to bring to the notice of a crowd of people a discourse that is totally filled with the whole majesty of the divine spirit.'

When Hammon had entered the sanctuary, and the fervour of the four men and the presence of God had filled this holy place, in due silence the minds and hearts of all hung upon the lips of Hermes, and divine love began to speak:

The One and the All

[2] 'O Asclepius, every human soul is immortal, but the nature of their immortality is not the same, for souls differ according to conduct and time.'

'Why, O Trismegistus? Is not every soul of one quality?'

'O Asclepius, how quickly you have broken from the just restraint of reason! For did I not say that all things are one and the one is all, since all these things were in the creator before he created them? Rightly is he said to be all, whose limbs are all things. And so, throughout this discourse, take care to be mindful of him who alone is all, or who is the creator of all. Everything comes from heaven into earth, into water, into air. Only fire, which is borne upwards, is life-giving. What moves downward serves it. Yet what moves down from on high is full of generative power; what moves upward gives nourishment. Only earth of all the elements remains within itself and is the receiver of every kind of form, and what it receives it returns.

'This therefore is the all, as you remember; it is the essence of the all and it is the all. The soul and the cosmos being embraced by Nature are set in movement by her with such diversity of quality, evident in all images, that countless forms are known to exist by the contrast of their qualities. Yet these forms are also united so that all things appear as one whole and from the one.

Cosmos, nature and the elements

[3] 'The elements, then, by which the whole cosmos has been formed are four: fire, water, earth, air. The cosmos is one, the soul is one, God is one.

'Now be entirely present, as far as your mind and ability are capable. For the knowledge of God is to be attained by a godlike concentration of consciousness. Such knowledge comes like a rushing river tumbling in flux from above to the depths beneath. By its headlong rush it outruns any effort we make as hearers, or even as teachers.

'Now heaven, the manifest god, directs all bodies, whose increase and decrease the sun and moon determine. But heaven and the soul itself, along with all that is in the cosmos are in turn governed by Him who has created them: this is God.

'From all the heavenly bodies just referred to, of which the same God is the ruler, continual influences are borne throughout the cosmos and throughout all ensouled classes and individual forms, because this is the nature of the cosmos. The cosmos has been prepared by God as a receptacle for forms of all kinds. Nature, then, impresses forms on matter by means of the four elements, and leads all things to heaven so that they will be pleasing in the sight of God.

Archetypes* and individual forms

[4] 'All beings dependent on the world above are divided into individual forms, as I am going to explain. The forms of all beings conform to their archetypes so that the archetype is the whole; the individual is a part of the archetype. Thus the archetype of gods will create from itself forms of gods; and so similarly with the archetype of daemons,* of men, of birds and the archetypes of all things which exist in the cosmos. They will all generate forms similar to themselves.

'There is another class of living being, a class without soul, which yet does not lack senses so that it benefits from good treatment, while it is weakened and injured by bad treatment. I am speaking of all those things which take life from the health of their roots in the ground and their shoots; their forms are scattered throughout the whole earth. Heaven itself is totally filled by God. But the archetypes of which I have spoken dwell in the space co-extensive with their forms; and insofar as they belong to their archetypes the forms are immortal. For the individual form is part of the archetype, as a man is part of humankind, so by necessity the individual conforms to the character of its archetype. But although all these archetypes are immortal, not all the individual forms are. In the case of the divine beings both the archetype itself and the individuals are immortal. For all the other classes immortality lies in the archetype. Although there is death for individual forms, life is preserved through the fecundity of reproduction. Thus the individual forms are mortal, the archetypes are not: man is mortal, humankind, immortal.

* See Translator's Note on pp. 51-2.

Associations

[5] 'However, the individual forms of all classes are mixed with all other classes; some of these were created early on; others were created from those which were made previously. Those which are created by gods, by daemons or by humans are the forms which bear the greatest similarity to their archetypes. It is impossible for bodies to be fashioned without the assent of the gods, or for individual forms to receive their shapes without the help of daemons, nor can beings without a soul be planted and cultivated without human beings. When any of the daemons pass from their own class into another form, and are perhaps joined to a form of the divine class, they are considered similar to gods because of their proximity and association. However, these daemons retain the quality of their own archetype and are called friends of humankind. The principle is the same with regard to humans, but it is more far-reaching. For the forms of humankind are many and are varied. Coming down from association with divine forms, in the way described, they make many unions with all other forms, and with most of them through necessity.

'On the same principle someone who, through divinely inspired religion, has joined himself to the gods in mind comes close to the gods. For it is by means of mind that a man becomes one with the gods, and similarly a man becomes one with the daemons who attaches himself to them. It follows that those beings are indeed human who are content with the middle position of their class, and all other human beings will be similar to the class belonging to the individuals with whom they associate.

Stature of Man

[6] 'Thus, O Asclepius, Man is a great miracle, a being to be adored and honoured. He passes into the nature of God as though he were God. He understands the race of daemons as he knows that he originates from the same source. He views with contempt that part of nature in himself which is human since he has put his entire trust in the divinity of the other part. How much happier is the nature of a man when it is tempered by self-control! He is united to the gods through a common divinity. He inwardly despises that part of himself by which he is earthbound. All other beings, to whom he knows he is necessary through divine dispensation, he binds to himself in a knot of love. He raises his sight to heaven while he takes care of the earth. Thus he is in the fortunate middle position: he loves those things that are below him and is beloved by the beings above. He quickly unites with the elements; through the sharpness of his mind he plumbs the depths of the sea. All things are open to him. The heavens do not seem too high, for he measures them by the skill of his mind as though he were very close to them. Foggy air never disturbs the direction of his attention; the dense earth is no obstacle to his work; no depth of water, however great, impairs his view. He is all things and he is the same everywhere.

'Of all kinds of beings those which are endowed with soul have roots reaching downwards from above, while those without soul reach upwards from a root which lives below. Some beings are nourished by two kinds of food, others by one kind alone. The two kinds of food by which beings endowed with soul exist are the food of the soul and the food of the body. The soul of the world is fed by unceasing movement. Bodies increase from water and earth, foods of the lower world [*mundi**]. The breath, by which all things are filled, mixes with all things and brings them to life. In human beings, intelligence is endowed with consciousness. This intelligence is the quintessence and is granted from heaven to human beings alone.

'Of all living beings it is in humans alone that consciousness provides the intelligence of divine reason; consciousness both raises and sustains this intelligence. But since I am being reminded to speak of consciousness I shall give you an account of it shortly. It is noble and most holy; no less than that of God Himself. But now I shall bring to a conclusion what I began.

Pure mind concealed by body

[7] 'For I was speaking of the union with the gods in the very beginning of things, by which humans alone fully enjoy the respect of the gods; that is, those men who have attained so much bliss that they perceive the divine consciousness in human intelligence; or rather the more than divine consciousness which is only in God and in human intelligence.'

'Is not consciousness the same in all men, O Trismegistus?'

'Not all men, O Asclepius, have attained true understanding, but through a rash impulse and without the true insight of reason most, pursuing an illusion, are deceived. This begets evil in minds and transforms the nature of the best living creature into that of a wild beast and makes it behave like a savage monster. But I shall give you a full account of consciousness and

* See Translator's Note on pp. 51-2.

all that is related to it when I speak of spirit. For of living beings Man alone is twofold: one part is single, which the Greeks term *"ousiodes"* and we call "the beauty of divine likeness"; the other is fourfold, which the Greeks term *"hulikon"* and we call "pertaining to matter". From this the body has been made, and it clothes what we have already said is divine in human beings. In this, the single divinity of pure mind is concealed, together with what is akin to it; this is the consciousness pertaining to the pure mind which remains wholly at rest within itself, as if enclosed by the wall of the body.'

'Why was it necessary, O Trismegistus, that Man be placed in the world [*mundo*] and not in that realm which is the abode of God where he might have lived in the highest bliss?'

'You are asking a good question, O Asclepius, and I pray God to give me the means of returning an answer to it. For since all things depend on his will, most certainly do these discussions which deal with absolute supremacy. Of this principle we are enquiring in our present conversation.

Twofold origin and role of humanity

[8] 'Then listen, Asclepius. The Lord and framer of all things, whom we rightly call God, made a god second to Himself who can be seen and apprehended by the senses. I do not call this second god susceptible to the senses on account of his being endowed with them; whether this is so or not I shall discuss at another time. But I so call him because he is discerned by the senses of those who do see. Since God made this divine being, which was the first to issue out of Himself and was the second after Himself, the sight of this being was beautiful to Him and

since it was entirely filled with the goodness of everything, He loved it as a child of His own divine nature.

'Having such power and such goodness He willed that there be another who could contemplate that being whom He had made from Himself. Therefore He made humankind to be an imitator of His reason and loving care. The will of God is the greatest perfection since willing and accomplishing are complete in the same instant of time. Thus He made human beings of His own essence. He perceived that they would not be able to love and care for all things unless He protected them with a material covering. So God sheltered them with a corporeal dwelling place and ordained the same for all human beings, and in just proportion He mixed and blended two natures into one. Thus God formed human beings of both spirit and body, that is, of both eternal and mortal nature, so that being thus formed they could do justice to their twofold origin: they could wonder at and adore the celestial, while they could also care for and manage the things on earth.

'But in speaking of mortal things, I do not only mean earth and water, two of the four elements which nature has made subject to human beings, but also those things which humans are responsible for doing in, or with, these elements: the cultivation of the earth itself, pasturage, building, ports, navigation, communication, trade. All these constitute the strongest bond between human beings, and between them and that part of the world [*mundi*] which is composed of water and earth.

'This earthly part of the world [*mundi*] is maintained by knowledge and practice of the arts and sciences, without which God has willed that it would not be brought to perfection. For what pleases God necessity obeys, as effect follows will; and it is not credible that what has pleased God will become displeasing to Him, since He knew long before, not only what would come to pass, but that it would please Him.

Veneration for God and care
for the cosmos

[9] 'But, Asclepius, I see how eagerly your quick mind hastens to hear how a man can make heaven, or what is within heaven, the object of his love and care. Then listen, O Asclepius. To love the God of heaven and all that pertains to Him is nothing but continual reverence for every thing. Such reverence has been offered by no other creature, divine or mortal, but only by human beings. By the wonder, adoration, praise and reverence of men heaven and its citizens are well pleased. Not undeservedly has the chorus of the Muses been sent down from Supreme God into the company of men so that the material world should not seem to be without order or lacking the sweetness of harmony. Indeed the sole Father of all sent down the Muses so that He might be honoured by the songs and praises of men, and that praise should not be lacking in heaven or the sweetness of harmony upon earth. And therefore a very few people endowed with a pure mind have been allotted the sacred trust of contemplating heaven. But there are those who from the confusion arising from their twofold nature have sunk back into the lower mind because of the weight of their body; such have been appointed to manage the elements and things associated with this lower world. Man, then, is a creature, but I do not say that he is inferior because he is in part mortal; rather on that account is he better adapted and more effectual for his specific

purpose, for this, his stature seems rather to have been increased by his mortality. Indeed, since he would not have been able to sustain both realms had he not been formed from the substance of both, he was so formed that he could care for the things of the earth and also love the divine.

In praise of Man

[10] 'And now, Asclepius, I desire that you apprehend the principle of what I am about to say, not only with keen attention but with liveliness of mind. Certainly, to most people this principle surpasses belief, but it may be understood by more spiritual minds as true and complete.

'And so I shall begin. The first God is the Lord of Eternity, the second is the cosmos, and the third is Man. God is the author of the cosmos and those that dwell therein. He is the governor of all things, together with Man, who is the governor of what has been compounded. Because Man looks to the whole, which is the proper object of his love and care, it follows that he is a jewel to the cosmos, as is the cosmos to him. Because of his divine composition, it seems Man has been called a world [*mundus*], but the Greek "*cosmos*" is more accurate. Man knows himself and he knows the cosmos, so that he remembers what is fitting for his role and recognises what is useful for him and what he should serve. While giving the greatest praises and thanks to God and reverencing his image, he is yet aware that he himself is the second image of God; for there are two images of God: the cosmos and Man. Hence it comes about that Man is a union of different parts. In part he is composed from soul and consciousness, spirit and reason by which he is divine. By these superior elements he seems able to ascend to heaven, but by the worldly part which consists of fire, earth, water and air he remains mortal upon earth lest he leave bereft and wasted all those things committed to his care. Thus mankind has been created in part divine and in part mortal, consisting of body.

Humans possessed by possessions

[11] 'Now the measure of this double being, that is of man, is firstly reverence for God, which is followed by goodness. For that goodness indeed seems perfect when it is protected by the virtue of despising the desire for everything else. All those things that are possessed because of the body's desire for earthly things are alien to the parts of a man which have kinship with the divine. They are well named possessions, since they were not born with us, but have come to be possessed by us later. That is why they are called possessions. All things of this kind are foreign to a man, including the body. Thus we must despise not only those things which we grasp at but also the very source within us from which the grasping comes. Thus the force of reason leads me to think that a man should be called a man only to the degree that, through contemplation of the divine, he looks down and sets little value on that part of him which is mortal, and which is joined to himself so that the lower world may be cared for.

'In order that both parts of man may be complete, note that both are formed of four elements. Man is equipped with pairs of hands and feet and other bodily members so that he may care for the lower, that is the earthly, world; but with the four elements of mind, consciousness, memory and foresight he may know all things divine and contemplate them. Hence it arises that he investigates the differences in things, their qualities, their effects and their quantities with uncertain search. Being held back by the weight and gross imperfection of the body, it follows that he cannot easily see into the true causes of natural things.

'Thus, if a man has been so created and fashioned, and given such duty and service by the most high God, if he maintains the world [*mundum*] in fine order, gives due reverence to God, and is fully obedient to his will in both these charges, what reward do you think he should be given? For as the world is the work of God, he who carefully maintains its beauty, and even increases it, joins his own work with the will of God, since by the dedication of his daily labour and care he gives order to the beauty which God created by his divine will. Should not the reward be that which our ancestors received, and which we ourselves desire in our deepest prayers, if only it should please divine goodness? That when we have completed our term of service, discharged our worldly duties, and have been freed from the bonds of mortality, God should restore us to our higher, that is divine nature, free from blemish and inviolable.'

Soul in a noose

[12] 'You speak with truth and justice, O Trismegistus.'

'This, then, is the reward for those who lead their life giving due reverence to God and loving care to the world [*mundo*]. It is very different for those who live unjustly and are denied a return to heaven. For they are obliged to undergo a shameful transmigration into bodies that are unworthy to hold the sacred spirit of man.'

'According to the tenor of your discourse, O Trismegistus, souls who hope for future immortality run great risks in this worldly life.'

'Yet to some what I have said seems incredible; to others a fable, and to others, perhaps, a matter for derision. For what is held dear in this life of the body is the fruit which is taken from possessions. But this is just what holds the soul in a noose, as it is said, so that a man sticks to that part of himself by which he is mortal, and the malice of this part, begrudging him immortality, does not allow him to acknowledge that part which is divine. Now I will speak to you as a prophet: after us there will be no one who has that simple love, which is the nature of philosophy. This consists in frequent contemplation and reverent worship by which alone the divinity may be known. Many destroy philosophy by their multifarious reasoning.'

'But how do they make philosophy incomprehensible, and how do they destroy it by multifarious reasoning?'

Philosophy destroyed by
multifarious reasoning

[13] 'In this way, Asclepius. By ingenious argument they mix it up with various kinds of incomprehensible study: arithmetic, music and geometry. But pure philosophy, which depends only on reverence for God, should attend to these other subjects just sufficiently to marvel at the knowledge that the heavenly bodies return regularly to the same predetermined positions, and that the course of their orbits is obedient to number. Philosophy should come to know the dimensions, qualities and quantities of the earth, the depths of the sea, the capacity of fire and the

effects and nature of all these things in order to admire, revere and praise the divine artistry and intelligence. To understand music is to comprehend the arrangement of all things, which is determined by divine proportion. By this proportion, which comes from the Supreme Artist, the arrangement of all individual things is transmuted into one which gives rise to the most beautiful and true harmony in the divine song.

God is neither begotten nor begets

[14] 'Those men who come after us will be deceived by cunning sophists and turned aside from true, pure and holy philosophy. To worship the Supreme Being with single mind and heart and to reverence what has been made of his substance, to render thanks to the divine will, which alone is infinitely full of the Good: this is a philosophy that has not been dishonoured by the perverse curiosity of the mind. But enough of this has been said.

'Let us now start to discuss spirit and what is akin to it. First there was God and *hulê*, which we take to be the Greek word for "matter" [*mundum*]. Spirit accompanied matter [*mundo*], or rather spirit was in matter [*mundo*] but it was in matter neither in the same way as it was in God, nor in the same way as those principles from which the cosmos came were in God. Those were not in being because they had not been brought forth, but they were already in God from whom they had the potential of birth. Not only are those beings said to be birthless which have not yet been born, but those which do not have the means of reproduction so that nothing can be born from them.

'Therefore, all beings that are, have within them the power of engendering and also of being engendered; from them arises

67

the potential of being born, even if those beings were born from themselves. For there is no doubt that those born from themselves naturally have the potential to be born. From such beings everything has been born. However, God is everlasting; the eternal God can neither be born nor ever could be born. That which is, which was, which ever will be, which is entirely from itself: that is the nature of God.

'Although *hulê* (matter), which is characteristic of the cosmos, and spirit do not seem to have been born from the beginning, nevertheless they have in themselves the power and natural capacity of being born and procreating. For the spring of fertility is a property of nature, which has the power and material of conception and birth within itself. Nature, then, has the power of generation by itself, without any other entity.

The unborn cosmos contains fertile nature

[15] 'Now we must turn to those beings which have the power to conceive only when joining with another, since the space of the cosmos with all that is in it, was clearly not born, but certainly has within itself the whole power of nature.

'Again, I say it is space in which all things are. All these things could not have existed if there had not been space to sustain them all (space must be provided for everything that is to be). Neither qualities, nor quantities, nor positions, nor effects could be discerned for things which were nowhere.

'Thus the cosmos, although it was not born, holds in itself the natures of all things, or rather it provides most fertile wombs for the conception of everything. This is the whole nature of matter: that it has the power of creation though it was not itself created.

Just as it is a quality in the nature of matter to multiply, so the same matter is equally fertile in multiplying evil.

How evils can be avoided

[16] 'Asclepius and Hammon, I have not said what is said by many: "Could God not have removed or averted evil from the nature of everything?" Absolutely no response should be given to these people. But for your sake I am going to proceed with what I have begun, and give you an answer. Those men say that God should have freed the world entirely from evil; yet it is in the world in such great measure that it seems like one of its limbs.

'Nevertheless Supreme God did foresee and guard against this in the most rational way possible when he deigned to bestow on the minds of men consciousness, knowledge and intelligence. For it is by these that we excel other living beings; by these alone can we avoid the deceits of evil, trickery and vice. A man guarded by divine intelligence and foreknowledge will by a mere glance of the eye avoid such things before he becomes involved in them. For the basis of knowledge resides in the Supreme Good.

'Everything in the cosmos is served and given energy by spirit, which, like a musical instrument or mechanical device, is subject to the will of the highest God. For now, let this be sufficient for us.

'He who is called the highest God and is known by mind alone, is the ruler and governor of the god who may be perceived by the senses. This "sensible" god comprehends in himself all space, the substance of everything and the whole nature of those that beget and create. He embraces whatever is, be it never so great.

Structure of the world

[17] 'All forms in the cosmos are moved and governed by spirit, each according to its own nature given to it by God, but *hulê* or matter is the receiver of them all. And of all these things God is the ruler. He is their movement and He is their meeting. He dispenses to all material things, whatever is necessary to each. What is more, he fills them all with spirit, breathed into them according to the natural capacity of each.

'The hollow rotundity of the world, which has the shape of a sphere, is itself invisible in its totality, by reason of its quality and its form. Choose any place whatsoever at the top of the sphere to look down below, from there you cannot see what is at the bottom. Because of this many believe the world to have the appearance and quality of a place. For it is only because of the forms of individual things whose images seem to be imprinted on the sphere that one believes it in a way to be visible, since it appears to be like a painting. But in reality it is in itself ever invisible. Hence it comes about that the bottom of the sphere, if it be a part of or place in the sphere, is called in Greek Hades, for *idein* in Greek means to see, and the bottom of the sphere cannot be seen. Hence also ideas are called forms, because they may be seen as forms. Therefore, too, the infernal regions are called in Greek Hades, because they cannot be seen, and in Latin *Inferi*, because they are at the bottom of the sphere.

These then are the first and most ancient causes; the head

and origin of everything; in them or through them or from them all things exist.'

The sun and the mind

[18] 'What really are all these things of which you speak, O Trismegistus?'

'One may say that the single substance within all individual forms, within each and every one, is the substance of the cosmos. Thus the cosmos nourishes bodies, and the spirit nourishes souls; but understanding is nourished by that heavenly gift by which alone mankind may be happy; not all men, but only a few: those whose mind is such that they can receive so great a benefit. As the world is lit by the light of the sun, so the human mind becomes clear by that other light; indeed more so. For whatever the sun illumines is sometimes deprived of that light by the interposition of the earth, the moon, and the arrival of night. But understanding, once it is joined with the human soul becomes a single substance through a total fusion, so that human minds of this kind are never impeded by the delusions of darkness. Hence it is rightly said that such understanding is the soul of the gods, but I say, not of all the gods, but only of the great or principal ones, and of these only the original.'

Gods and stars

[19] 'What gods do you say are at the very head of things, or the source of primordial causes, O Trismegistus?'

'I am putting great things before you and unveiling divine mysteries. Before I make a start I implore the favour of heaven.

There are many classes of gods of whom some are subtle and others sensory. The first are so described not because they are considered to be beyond our apprehension; indeed, we apprehend them better than the ones we call visible, as the discourse will show, and if you give your attention, you will be able to see clearly. For this discourse is sublime and the more divine for standing beyond the minds and purposes of men. If you do not hear the words of the speaker with attentive obedience the discourse will fly over you and flow round you, or rather, it will flow back and mingle again with the waters of its own source.

'There are then gods who are the leaders of all the individual gods. The other gods follow these leaders, of whom the first is pure being. These sensory gods, true to their twofold origin, accomplish all things through their sensory nature; each works through another, and each illumines his own work.

'The ruling principle or essence of the heavens (whatever is understood by that term) is Jupiter, for it is through the agency of heaven that Jupiter gives life to all beings. The essence of the sun is light, for the goodness of its light is poured out upon us through its orb. The thirty-six, who are called the horoscopes,* that is the constellations which are always fixed in the same place, have as their essence him who is called *Pantomorphon*, or omniform, who gives different forms to different individuals. The seven spheres, as they are called, have as their essence her who is called Fortune or Fate through which all things are

---

*Each of the thirty-six horoscopes represents one third of each of the twelve signs; each sign signifies a constellation (Aries, Taurus, etc.). The seven spheres are the apparent orbits of the seven planets visible to the naked eye as viewed from the earth: Sun, Moon, Mercury, Venus, Mars, Jupiter, Saturn.

changed by the law of nature. This law is absolutely unchanging, yet all things are varied by continual movement.

'Air is the instrument or mechanism of all things, through which everything is accomplished, and the essence of this is ...
[*text missing here*]

'Since this is so, all things reach out to one another and are connected from lowest to highest. They are connected to what is moving towards them and to everything that appertains to them.

'The mortal is joined to the immortal, and that which is perceptible to the senses to that which is not. In fact the whole creation, not being a multiplicity, but one, obeys Him who is the Supreme Ruler and the Supreme Lord. For all things depend upon the one and all things flow from the one. When seen from a distance they appear to be infinite, but viewed as a whole they are in truth one, though one could say two: that from which all proceeds and that by which all is made, that is the substance from which all is made. By His will and His assent everything else comes into existence.'

The name of God

[20] 'Once more, what is this teaching, O Trismegistus?'

'It is this, Asclepius. God, or Father, or Lord of all, or He whom men call by any other name that is more holy and reverend, should be held sacred by us because of our intelligence. When we contemplate so great a divine spirit we shall find we cannot name him precisely by any of these names. For the spoken word is just this: a sound from the air when it is struck by breath, expressing the whole will and thought of a man; what from the senses he has perhaps understood in his mind. The nature of his name is his whole substance ordered into a few limited and compressed syllables. It is thus in man the necessary connection between voice and ears. But the name of God is the totality of sense, of breath, of air and of all things in these or through these or from these.

'Therefore I do not have any hope that the creator of the majesty of the whole, the Father and Lord of all, can have a single name, even one composed of many names. Indeed, He has no name, or rather He has every name since He is one and He is all, so that one must call all things by His name or give Him the name of all things. Thus, as He is single, and as He is all, He is filled with the potency of both sexes. Being ever pregnant with His own will, throughout all time He brings forth whatever He has wished to create. His will is nothing but the Good.

'This same Good in all things is born naturally from His divinity so that all things should be as they are, and as they have been, and that they should be able to empower all things that may come to be, with the ability to give birth from themselves. So, Asclepius, the explanation has been given to you as to why and how all things come into being.'

The mystery of love

[21] 'What, are you saying that God is of both sexes, O Trismegistus?'

'Not only God, Asclepius, but every being that has a soul and also those that do not. It is not possible for any one of them to exist without being fruitful. For if fecundity were withdrawn from all living beings it would be impossible for them to continue for all time to be what they are; I tell you that Nature holds and preserves within herself everything that has been brought into being. Both sexes are full of the creative force, as is the union of the two. In truth their union is incomprehensible. This you may rightly call Cupid or Venus or you may use both names.

'Therefore take this to heart, for assuredly nothing is more true or more evident than this: that the mystery of eternal procreation was conceived by God and bestowed upon all creatures by Him, the Lord of all Nature, in which Nature dwell the greatest tenderness, joy, gladness, longing and divine love. I would explain how great is the force and how compelling the power of this mystery, were it not that each one of us knows this from reflection on his own innermost feelings. For if you observe that final moment when, through continuous interaction, we come to the point where each gender pours its fertile power into the other and the other eagerly seizes it and hides it within, then by the mutual union at this moment the woman acquires the strength of the man and the man relaxes in female passivity.

'The performance of this sweet and vital mystery takes place in secret lest the divinity of Nature that arises from the union of sex were compelled by the mocking and ignorant to feel ashamed if the act were performed openly; much worse still, if it were seen by the enemies of religion.

Humans and gods

[22] 'There are not many, indeed so few religious men or women in the world [*mundo*] that they can be counted. Thus it is that evil remains among the people through the lack of wisdom and

knowledge of what really exists. For it is from the intelligence of divine reason, through which all things are constituted, that contempt for the vices of the whole world [*mundi*] is born, and this contempt is also their cure. But through continuing lack of experience and absence of knowledge all the vices grow strong and do irreparable damage to the soul which, being infected by them, swells up as if from poison, except in the case of those who have found the sovereign remedy: knowledge and intelligence. Therefore, even if all this will be of use only to a few people, it is worth pursuing and finishing the discussion as to why the Deity considered human beings alone worthy to receive from Him His own intelligence and knowledge.

'So listen. After God the Father and Lord had brought forth the gods he formed man, in part from the corruption of matter, but in equal part from the divine. The imperfections of matter then remained mixed within bodies, together with other imperfections derived from the food and nourishment which we take through necessity, as do all living beings. It is therefore inevitable that the desires arising from greed, and other vices of the mind steal into human souls.

'As for the gods, they are composed of the purest part of Nature, and they do not need the supports of reason and knowledge. For them immortality and the vigour of eternal youth are themselves intelligence and knowledge. Yet lest they should ever become separated from these, to safeguard the unity of God's design He established the rule of Necessity drawn up as a law in accordance with eternal law. Of all living beings He recognised man alone as having reason and knowledge through which he can turn away and distance from himself the vices of the body. He presented man with the hope of immortality and the will to reach it. So God made man both good, and capable of immortality, because of his two natures: the divine and the mortal. Through God's will it was ordained that man was thus made superior both to the gods, who are formed only of an immortal nature, and to all other creatures. Because of this man is united to the gods in kinship and he therefore worships them through religion and through purity of mind. For their part the gods look down on all human affairs with tender love and take care of them.

Man the maker of gods

[23] 'But that may be said only of the few men who are endowed with a faithful mind. Of those with a liking for vice let nothing be said lest this highly spiritual discourse be dishonoured by thinking of them.

'And since I have spoken of the kinship and fellowship of men with the gods, Asclepius, acknowledge the power and strength of Man. Just as the Lord and Father, or God (his greatest name) is the creator of the heavenly gods, so Man is the maker of the gods in temples, who are content to be close to human beings. Man not only receives light, but he gives it. Not only does Man progress towards God, but he forms gods. Do you wonder at this, Asclepius, or do you doubt as most people do?'

'I am astounded, O Trismegistus, but I willingly assent to your words and regard Man as most fortunate inasmuch as he has attained such great happiness.'

'And he, who is the greatest of all creatures, is justly worthy of admiration. Everyone agrees that the race of gods clearly sprang from the purest part of Nature, and their symbols are simply heads which represent the whole being. But the forms of gods which men create are taken from two natures: from the divine, which is purer and far more god-like; and from that which is within men, that is, from matter. Having been formed from such matter, they are not represented by heads alone, but by the whole body with all its members. Thus humanity is always reminded of its own nature and origin as it continues to represent divinity in this way. So just as the Father and Lord has made the eternal gods to be similar to Himself, so humanity has made its gods in the likeness of its own features.'

Disaster foretold

[24] 'Are you speaking of statues, O Trismegistus?'

'Yes, statues, Asclepius. Do you see how you lack faith? These statues are made alive by consciousness, and they are filled with breath. They do mighty deeds. They have knowledge of the future which they predict through oracles, prophets, dreams and in many other ways. They bring illnesses to men and cure them. They give sadness and happiness according to merit. Do you not realise, Asclepius, that Egypt is the image of heaven; or to speak more precisely, all things which are set in motion and regulated in heaven have been transferred, or have descended, into Egypt? More truthfully still, our land is the temple of the whole cosmos.

'Yet since the wise should know all that is to come, it is right that you should not be ignorant of something else. A time will come when it appears that the Egyptians have worshipped God with pure mind and sincere devotion in vain. All their holy worship will turn out to be without effect and will bear no fruit.

For the gods will withdraw from earth to heaven and Egypt will be deserted. The land which used to be the seat of religion will be abandoned by the gods and become void of their presence. Not only will foreigners, pouring into the region and covering this land, neglect religion, but what is worse, religion, duties to the gods and divine worship will be prohibited with penalties prescribed by so-called laws. This holy land, this home of sanctuaries and temples, will all be filled with sepulchres and the dead. O Egypt, Egypt, only stories of your religion will survive, and these your children will not believe. Only words carved in stone will narrate your pious deeds. Scythians, Indians or other such will inhabit Egypt; it will be peopled by barbarian neighbours. The gods will return to heaven and abandon men, who will then all die. Thus Egypt, deprived of gods and men, will become a desert.

'Now I speak to you, most holy river. I tell of your future. You will be filled with a torrent of blood, right up to your banks, and these you will burst through. Not only will your sacred waters be polluted with blood, but your banks will burst open, and the dead will far outnumber the living. Anyone who survives will be recognised only by his language as Egyptian. From his actions one would take him to be a foreigner.

Greater evils

[25] 'Why do you weep, Asclepius? Egypt herself will be led into much worse things than these, and she will be sunk in greater evils. This once holy land which had such great love for the gods, where alone they deservedly fixed their seat on earth because of her devotion, for she taught men religion and piety, will

become an example of the most ferocious cruelty. Then to men, tired of living, the cosmos will no longer seem an object of wonder or something to be reverenced.

'Nothing better was, is or ever will be seen than the goodness of this whole cosmos, yet it will become a danger and a burden to men. Because of this people will no longer love, but come to despise it: this inimitable work of God, this glorious creation, this perfection formed with such variety of images, this instrument of God's will, who in his work gives favour without partiality. This cosmos, a world of many forms, brings everything to unity, the unity of the all. It is a cosmos which can be revered, praised and finally loved by those able to see it. The dark will indeed be preferred to the light, and death thought better than life. No one will have any regard for heaven and a spiritual person will be deemed mad, and a materialist, wise. An angry man will be considered strong and the most evil regarded as good.

'All the teaching about the soul that I have explained to you is that the soul is born immortal or expects to attain immortality. This teaching will not only be laughed at, but considered an illusion. It will be held as a capital offence, believe me, for a man to have given himself over to reverence of the divine mind. New rights will be created. There will be new laws. Nothing holy, nothing religious, nothing worthy of heaven or the gods which inhabit it, will either be heard or believed.

'How grievous will be the withdrawal of gods from men! Only the evil angels will remain. Mingling with humanity they will force these wretches into all the evils of violence: wars, robbery, fraud and all those things which are contrary to the nature of souls. In those days the earth will not be stable, nor will the sea be navigable. Heaven will not be traversed by the stars, for the course of the stars will cease in the sky. Every divine voice will of necessity be stopped. The fruits of the earth will wither, and the land will no longer be fertile. The very air will hang heavy in lifeless torpor.

Restoration

[26] 'Such will be the old age of the world: irreligion, disorder, and unreason concerning all that is good. When all this happens, O Asclepius, the Lord and Father, the god who is first in power and governor under God who is the One, will consider the conduct and wilful deeds of men. Through his will, which is the goodness of God, he will take a stand against these evils and against the universal corruption. He will restrain error and every malign influence. Either he will dissolve all this in a flood, or consume it by fire, or destroy it through disease and pestilence spread through different lands. Finally he will restore the world to its ancient beauty, so that it may again appear worthy of reverence and wonder, and also that God the creator and restorer of so great a work may be worshipped by people then living with continual hymns of praise and benediction. By these events the world will be reborn. There will be a return of all that is good, a sacred and spiritual re-establishment of Nature herself compelled by the course of time through that will, which is and was, without beginning and without end. For the will of God has no beginning, but remains the same; as it is now, so will it always be. For the nature of God is the purpose of his will.'

'And the highest Good is this purpose, O Trismegistus?'

'Will is born from purpose, Asclepius, and acts of willing from will. And God wills nothing in excess, for he has unlimited abundance of everything and he wills what he has. He wills everything good, and he has everything that he wills. Therefore all that he purposes and wills is good. Such is God, and the world a reflection of that Good.'

God and the gods

[27] 'The world is good, O Trismegistus?'

'It is good, Asclepius, as I will teach you. For just as God husbands and distributes to all individuals and classes all the good things which are in the world [*mundo*], senses, soul and life, so the world [*mundus*] apportions and provides all those things which seem good to mortals: the succession of births in due season, the germination, growth and ripening of the fruits of the earth and similar things. Throughout all this God, abiding above the vault of the highest heaven, is everywhere observing all that is around. For there is a place beyond heaven where there are no stars, far removed from all corporeal things.

'The god who is the dispenser of life and whom we call Jupiter, has a realm between heaven and earth. As for the earth and the sea, they are ruled by Jupiter Plutonius. It is he who nourishes mortal creatures and all that bears fruit. The fruits, trees and soil are enlivened by the power of all these gods. But there are other gods whose powers and actions are apportioned to everything which exists. As for those gods who rule the earth, they will be dispersed and then settled in a town at the very extremity of Egypt, which will be founded towards the setting sun, and to which the whole race of mortals will hasten both by land and sea.'

'But where are these gods now, O Trismegistus?'

'They reside in a great city on the Libyan mountain. And that is enough on the subject for the time being.

Death

'We must now discuss what is immortal and what is mortal, for hope and fear of death torment many who are ignorant of true reason. Death is the result of the dissolution of the body when it is worn out by toil and the days are over in which the parts of the body were fit for living use in a single entity. Thus the body dies when it ceases to be able to carry out the living functions of a man. This then is death: the dissolution of the body and the extinction of bodily senses. It is pointless to be concerned about this. But it is necessary to be concerned about other things that ignorance and human disbelief discount.'

'What is it, O Trismegistus, that human beings ignore or believe cannot exist?'

Life after death

[28] 'Listen, Asclepius. When the soul has departed from the body it will come under the power of a most potent spirit who will examine its merits and judge it. When that spirit has discerned that the soul is pious and just, he permits it to remain in the region which it merits. But if he sees it covered with the stains of crime, and oblivious of its vices, he hurls it from the heights to the depths, delivering it to storms and whirlwinds, to the ever contending elements of air, fire and water so that it is caught between heaven and earth, continually buffeted in dif-

ferent directions by the turbulence of the world. Thus eternity for such a soul is an evil in that by immortal judgement it is sentenced to endless torture. Know then, to avoid this we must stand in awe at such a fate, we must be fearful and guard against it. The disbelievers after their crimes will be forced to believe, not from words but from experience, not from threats but from the agony of punishment.'

'Then they are not punished by human law alone, Trismegistus?'

'In the first place, Asclepius, everything which exists on earth is mortal. Now those beings which live according to the laws of the body depart from life by reason of the same laws. They all submit to punishments according to the merits of their life or the crimes of which they are guilty. But the punishments are worse after death since they may have been able to conceal things during life. Punishments for all these things will be given by the all-knowing divinity in exact measure to the nature of the crimes.'

The just protected

[29] 'Who are worthy of the greatest punishments, O Trismegistus?'

'They are those who have been condemned by human laws and thus suffered a violent death, for they seem not to have returned their life to Nature as the payment of a debt, but to have been deservedly punished. However, the just man is protected by his faith in God and by intense spiritual practice. God protects such men from every evil, for He is the Father and Lord of everyone. He alone is all. He freely reveals Himself to everyone, not as though He were in some place, or possessed of some particular quality or greatness, but by illuminating man with the single intelligence of his mind. When the shades of error have been dispersed from a man's heart and the light of truth has been perceived, that man joins himself with all his powers to the divine intelligence. Through the love of this he is set free from that part of his nature by which he is mortal and he receives firm faith in future immortality. This, then, is the difference between good and evil men. Every good man becomes illumined by his piety, by his spirituality, by his wisdom and by his worship and veneration of God. Everything is seen by the light of true reason, as though by the physical eyes. The assurance of his faith excels that of other men just as the sun excels the light of the other stars. For the sun illumines the other heavenly bodies less by the brightness of its light, than by its divinity and purity.

The Sun a second god

'Believe that this Sun is a second god, O Asclepius, who rules all things and fills all beings in the cosmos with light, both those with a soul and those without a soul. For if the cosmos is a being which lives for ever; if it was, is and will be, nothing in it is subject to death. Since each part lives for ever (as it does), and is always within that same cosmos, and that single being is ever-living, there is no place here for death. If therefore of necessity this cosmos is everlasting, it must itself be the fullness of life and eternity. As the cosmos is everlasting, so the Sun is the everlasting ruler of all things that live and of their very life force; it gives forth life and does so continually. It is god of the living and of all things which have the potential of life in the cosmos. It is the everlasting ruler and dispenser of life itself. Yet it has given life but once. Life is provided to all living beings by eternal law in a way I shall describe.

God and eternity

[30] 'The cosmos is moved within the very principle of life that comes from Eternity: and its place is within this living eternity. Because it is surrounded by the ever-living force of Eternity, as if held by it, it will never cease to move, nor will it ever be destroyed. The cosmos itself is the dispenser of life to everything and it is where everything ruled by the Sun exists. The movement of the cosmos comes from a twofold operation. It receives life from outside, from Eternity, and it gives life to everything within it, diversifying it according to numbers and times, which are fixed and determined by the operation of the sun and the course of the stars. For the whole cycle of time has been written in divine law. Time on earth is marked by the quality of the air and the variation of heat and cold, but celestial time by the return of the constellations to the same places in the course of their circuits. The cosmos is the container of time, and by its course and movement the cosmos is kept alive. Time is kept in being by ordained law. Through the process of alternation, order and time are responsible for the renewal of everything which is in the cosmos.

'Since all things are thus ordered nothing is still, nothing is settled, nothing is immovable that comes into being, whether celestial or terrestrial; only God is excepted; He alone. For He is in Himself and from Himself and round Himself. He is all. He is complete and He is perfect. He is his own enduring stillness and He cannot be moved by any impulse from His place, since all things are in Him and He alone is in all things; unless anyone were bold enough to say that He moves in Eternity; but it is more accurate to say that He is motionless Eternity itself into which the movement of all cycles returns and from which the movement of all cycles begins.

Eternity and time

[31] 'It follows that God has been for ever still and so has Eternity, which is similar to Him. Eternity contained within itself a cosmos not yet born which we rightly say is sensory. This cosmos has been brought into being as an image of Eternity, and as an imitator of Eternity. Moreover, time has the power and nature of its own stillness since although it is always in motion, it necessarily turns upon itself. Although Eternity is still, immovable and unchanging, the course of time (which does move) always returns to Eternity, and that movement is directed by the law of time itself. Thus it happens that Eternity which alone is still through time, exists itself in time; all movement seems to take place in time.

'Thus it is that the stillness of Eternity is in movement, and that the movement of time is made still by the unchanging law which governs its course. And thus it is credible that God is moved within Himself, by the same immobility. Indeed, in the unlimited stillness itself movement is unmoving, for the law of the unlimited is itself unmoving. Such then is the nature of this being: imperceptible, unlimited, unthinkable, immeasurable. It can neither be held in nor taken away; nor can it be hunted down. Where it is, whither it goes, whence it came, how or what it is, cannot be known. For it is moved within supreme stillness and yet this stillness is within itself; be it God or Eternity or both, or one in the other, or both in both. On account of this, Eternity is without limitation of time. But although time can be defined by number, by alternation, by periodic return through revolution, time is eternal. Thus both appear infinite, both eternal. Inasmuch as stillness is without movement, so that it can support all that moves, it is justly sovereign by virtue of its constancy.

Divine and human consciousness

[32] 'Thus God and Eternity are the origin of all that is. But the cosmos, because it is in movement, does not have primacy, for its movement precedes its stillness, since its unchanging constancy is based on the law of everlasting movement.

'Consciousness in its totality, being similar to divinity, is itself motionless, yet it moves itself within its own stillness. Consciousness is holy, uncorrupt and eternal and whatever can be named higher than that, if anything can be. Eternity abides in the very truth of the Supreme God. It is totally full of all sensory forms and of all knowledge. It abides, as it were, with God. Cosmic consciousness is a receptacle of all sensory forms and of all branches of knowledge. Man's consciousness depends on the tenacity of his memory, that is, the memory of all that he has experienced. But the divine consciousness in its descent reaches as far as the human being. For Supreme God did not wish divine consciousness to be poured into all living beings, lest it should be shamed at being joined to other creatures.

'Now the intelligence of human consciousness, be it of whatever kind or capacity, consists totally in the memory of past
events, and through the tenacity of this memory it has become
the ruler of the Earth. But the intelligence of Nature can be
attained through the capacity of cosmic consciousness from
everything which is subject to the senses in the cosmos. The
consciousness of Eternity, which comes next, has also been
bestowed and its quality made known by the sensory world. But
the intelligence and quality of the consciousness belonging to
the Supreme God is truth alone. Of this not even the faintest
outline of a shadow may be seen on Earth. For where anything
is known through the dimension of time there is falsehood.

'Where you see birth, there you see delusion. So you see,
Asclepius, where we stand, what we are engaged upon and what
we dare to attain. But to you, O Highest God, I give thanks, for
Thou hast illumined me with the light of the Divinity that is to
be seen. And you, O Tat, Asclepius and Hammon, hold these
divine mysteries in the secrecy of your heart. Cover them with
silence and conceal them with quiet.

'Now there is this difference between intelligence and consciousness: through concentration of mind our intelligence
comes to understand and discern the nature of the consciousness pertaining to the world, but the intelligence of the world
comes to know Eternity and the gods above. And so it happens
to us men that, as if through a mist, we come to see what is in
heaven, as far as this is possible through the limited nature of
human consciousness. Although this power of ours to discern
such exalted things is very limited, it is quite unlimited when
it sees through the grace of pure consciousness.

There is no void

[33] 'As for the void which now seems so important to so many people, I consider that there is no void, there never could have been a void and there never will be a void. All parts of the cosmos are totally full, so that the cosmos itself is full and complete with bodies that differ in both form and quality; and each has its own appearance and size. One may be larger than another and one smaller; one may be more dense and another more subtle. Those that are more dense are more easily seen, as are those which are larger. Those that are smaller or subtler can only be seen with difficulty and sometimes not at all. These we know of only by keen attention. Hence many people believe that these are not bodies, but empty places, which is impossible.

'And the same would be true of space which is said to exist outside the cosmos (that is, if it does exist, which I do not believe). I consider that space would be full of beings which can be apprehended only by mind, that is, of beings similar to its own divinity. Thus this cosmos which we say is perceptible by the senses is totally full of bodies and of beings which accord with its own nature and quality. We do not see all their true forms; indeed, some appear excessively large, and others far too small. It is either owing to the extent of the intervening space, or to the feebleness of our sight that they so appear to us, and because of their excessive smallness they are believed by many not to exist at all. I speak now of spirits which I believe dwell with us, and demi-gods which live between the purest part of the air above us and those realms where there is no fog and no clouds and no disturbance arising from any celestial body.

'Take care, then, Asclepius, not to speak of anything as void, unless you say what it is void of, for instance, that it is void of fire or of water or similar things. For even if one happens to see an object, whether small or great, which seems to be void of these things, though it may appear empty, it cannot be empty of spirit and air.

The sensory world

[34] 'The same should be said about "place": it is a word that has no meaning on its own. For "place" only has meaning in relation to that of which it is the place. If this principle is removed, then the meaning of the word is incomplete. That is why we rightly speak of the place of water, or of fire, or of other similar things. For just as it is impossible for anything to be empty, so one cannot know what place is on its own. If one were to imagine a place without an object of which it is the place, then the place would appear empty, which I do not believe is possible in the cosmos. If nothing is empty, then what place is cannot be known unless you add the dimensions of length, breadth and height to it, as you do to human bodies.

'Since this is how things are, O Asclepius, and you who are present, know that the causal world of mind, discernible only by contemplation, is incorporeal, and that nothing corporeal can be mingled with its nature, nothing distinguished by quality, quantity or number, for in it there is nothing of that kind.

'As for this cosmos, which is called sensory, it is the receptacle of all the qualities or substances of all the sensory forms and bodies, none of which can be given life without God. For God is everything. Everything comes from Him and depends on His will. This whole is good, beautiful, wise and unique; perceived and understood by Him alone, without whom nothing ever was, is, or will be. All things are from Him, in Him and through Him: the various qualities and their many guises, the vast sizes beyond all means of measure, and forms of every kind. For these, if you understand them, O Asclepius, you will give thanks to God. If you give your attention to the whole, you will come to understand that in truth the sensory world and all within it is from the world above and is covered by that as if by a garment.

Individuals differ within an archetype

[35] 'Every class of being, O Asclepius, whether mortal or immortal, rational or irrational, whether endowed with a soul or without a soul, each will have the characteristics belonging to its archetype. And although each being has the whole form of its archetype, yet each individual of the same form differs from the others. Although archetypal man has one form, so that a man may be known as such by his appearance, nevertheless within that same form individual men differ from each other.

'For the ideal form, being divine, is incorporeal, as is everything which is apprehended by mind. Since therefore there are two elements of which forms consist, the corporeal and incorporeal, it is impossible for any form to come into existence exactly similar to any other form at different points of time and place. Indeed, they are changed as often as the hour has moments, during the turning of the circle in which He dwells, who has all forms, whom we have called God. So the ideal form is permanent and brings forth from itself as many and as diverse images as the revolution of the cosmos has moments, for the universe itself changes in the course of its revolution, but the ideal form itself neither changes nor revolves. Thus the forms of every class persist but there are differences within the same form.'

Changes in appearance

[36] 'And does the cosmos change its appearance, O Trismegistus?'

'O Asclepius, you seem to have been asleep while all this was being explained to you. For what is the cosmos in reality? And of what is it made? Simply of everything that has been brought into being? So what you are really enquiring about is the sky, the earth and the elements. And what changes in appearance more often than these? The sky is either moist or dry, cold or hot, clear or murky. These appearances are all within the one form of heaven, and they frequently interchange.

'The earth too continually changes in appearance as when it brings forth fruit and then nourishes what it has brought forth, when it yields the varied qualities and different quantities of its fruits, and determines their stages and courses of development, and above all, when it produces the qualities, scents, tastes and appearances of trees, flowers and berries. Fire brings about many changes that are worthy of a deity. Reflections of the sun and moon also present every kind of form. In a way they are similar to the reflections of our mirrors which return images of their originals with comparable splendour.

Animation of statues

[37] 'But let this be enough on such things.

'Let us return to man and reason. Because of the divine gift of reason, man is said to be an animal with reason. Even though what has already been said about man is a cause of wonder, it is less wonderful than this gift of reason. This merits more admiration than anything else: that man has been able to discover his divine nature and make it manifest.

'Because our sceptical ancestors erred greatly in their opinion of the gods and gave no attention to worship and divine religion, they invented an art by which they could create gods. To this discovery they added a complementary power drawn from the nature of the cosmos, making the two work together. Since they could not make souls they summoned the souls of demons or angels and implanted them into images with sacred and divine rites. By means of these they were able to create idols having both good and evil powers.

'Your grandfather, O Asclepius, was the founder of medicine, to whom a temple has been consecrated on the mountain of Libya, near the Shore of the Crocodiles, in which lies his terrestrial part, that is, his body. The rest, or rather the whole of him, if manhood consists in the consciousness of life, has gone to heaven to better advantage. For now through his divine spirit he still furnishes the sick with every kind of aid which previously he used to provide through the art of medicine. Is it not true that my grandfather Hermes, after whom I am named, resides in his eponymous town whence he aids and cures all those who come to him from every land? We know how much good Isis, the consort of Osiris can do, when well disposed, and how much harm when she is angry. It is easy to anger the terrestrial and material gods since they have been made and put together by men, from both divine and human natures. On a similar principle some living beings are called sacred by the

Egyptians, and their souls, which were sanctified while they were alive, are worshipped in particular cities. Thus the Egyptians live by their laws and are called by their names. It seems to be for this reason, Asclepius, that these beings are worshipped and revered in some cities, but are considered differently by others. On this account the cities of Egypt habitually make war on each other.'

Terrestrial gods

[38] 'What is the nature of these gods which are considered to be terrestrial, Trismegistus?'

'O Asclepius, it is derived from herbs, stones and spices which have in themselves the power of divinity in Nature. Because of this these gods are delighted by frequent sacrifices, hymns, praises and sweet sounds in tune with the celestial harmony. Thus what comes from the heavens can be enticed by the frequent use of heavenly means to happily endure long periods of time, content with humanity. Thus man is the creator of gods. And do not think that the actions of these earthly gods are random, Asclepius. The celestial gods dwell in the highest realm of heaven. Each one fulfils and protects the order of beings which has been assigned to him. But these gods of ours help us as though they were loving parents: either they attend to particular matters, or they foretell the future through lot and divination, or they provide certain things, and by these means they come to help human beings, each in his own way.'

Destiny, necessity and order

[39] 'Then what part in the scheme of things do Destiny or the Fates play, O Trismegistus? Do not the celestial gods govern universals, while the terrestrial gods look after individual things?'

'What we call Destiny, O Asclepius, is the Necessity of all events which take place and these are ever bound to herself by the links of a chain. Thus she is either the cause of everything, or she is the Supreme God, or she is formed from that God as the second god, or she is the sustained order of all things celestial and terrestrial, which is established by divine laws. Thus Destiny and Necessity are inseparably bonded together; the first of these is Destiny which begets the seeds of everything, but Necessity brings those seeds to fruition which depend on Destiny for their inception. Order follows these two; Order being the interweaving and timing of all things that must come to pass. For nothing is composed without Order, and this cosmos is complete in every detail. For the universe itself is moved by Order and is established wholly upon Order.

[40] 'There are then these three: Destiny, Necessity and Order. They have arisen in the first place from the will of God, who governs the cosmos by his law and through divine reason. God has therefore entirely removed from them all willing and non-willing. They are neither moved by anger, nor deflected by favour, but serve the Necessity of eternal reason; this Eternity is ineluctable, unmoving and indissoluble.

'First then, is Destiny, which having, as it were, cast the seed, produces the offspring of all that is to come. Necessity follows, by whom all things are compelled by force into activity. Order is third, which maintains the connection of what has been ordained by Destiny and Necessity. Such then is Eternity; it neither begins nor ceases to be and it is turned in the everlasting motion of its revolution by fixed and immutable law. Its parts are always rising and falling alternately, so that as the times change those same parts which had fallen, rise again. Thus revolving circularity is its principle, so that things are so well bound to it that you do not know where the beginning is, if there is a beginning, since everything always seems both to precede and follow itself. Moreover consequence or fate are mixed into everything in the cosmos.

'As much has been said to you on each of these subjects as a human being can express and the Supreme Deity both wills and allows. It only remains for us to return to the care of the body, blessing God and praying to Him. For in discussing divine matters we have, I may say, sufficiently filled ourselves with the food of the soul.'

Prayer of thanksgiving

[41] Leaving the sanctuary of the temple they began to pray to God, having first turned towards the South, for anyone wishing to ask anything of God at sunset should face that direction, just as at sunrise one should face East. As they began their prayer, Ascelpius said in a low voice,

'O Tat, do you think that we should suggest to your father that he order frankincense and perfumes to be used when we say our prayer to God?'

When Trismegistus heard him he was stirred and said, 'Give us a far better omen than that, Asclepius. It is like sacrilege to burn frankincense and other things when you pray to God; for

97

He lacks nothing, who is Himself all things or in whom are all things. Rather let us adore Him in giving thanks, since this is the finest incense for God: that thanks be given Him by mortals.

'We render you thanks, most high and potent God, for it is only by your grace that we have come to the light of your knowledge. Holy and reverend is your name, the one name by which God alone is to be praised according to the religion of our fathers. We do indeed thank you since you deign to give all beings your paternal care, your religion and your love, and even sweeter, upon us you have bestowed these powers: perception, reason and intelligence; perception, that we may recognise you; reason, that we may follow up our intuition, and knowledge, that in knowing you we may find joy.

'Having been saved by your divine power we rejoice, because you have shown yourself to us in your totality. We rejoice, because while we are still in these bodies, you deign to consecrate us for Eternity. This is the only way human beings have of giving thanks: to acknowledge your majesty. We have known you and the supreme light by conscious intelligence alone. We understand you, O true life of life, O fertile womb of all that has come into being. O eternal steadfastness, we have known you in your conception of the whole of abundant Nature. In every prayer through which we reverence the Good of all good, we plead only for this: that you may wish us to continue to serve you in the love of your knowledge and that we may never be separated from this kind of life.

'Desirous of these things we turn to a repast that is pure, and undefiled by the flesh of animals.'

Bibliography

Allen, M.J.B. and Rees, V. (eds), *Marsilio Ficino: His Theology, His Philosophy, His Legacy* (Brill, Leiden, 2001).

Camplani, A., 'Riferimenti biblici nella litteratura ermetica', *Annali di storia dell' esegesi* 10/2 (1993), 375-425.

Clarke, Emma C., Dillon, John M. and Herschbelt, Jackson P. (trs), Iamblichus, *De mysteriis* (Brill, Leiden, 2004).

Copenhaver, B.P., *Hermetica,* an English translation of the *Corpus Hermeticum* and *Asclepius* (Cambridge University Press, Cambridge, 1992).

De Durand, G.-M., 'Un traité hermétique conservé en arménien', *Revue de l'Histoire des Religions* 190 (1976), 55-72.

Eckhart (Meister), *Selected Writings*, tr. Oliver Davies (Penguin Classics, London, 1994).

Emerson, R.W., *Selected Writings of Ralph Waldo Emerson*, ed. B. Atkinson (Modern Library edition, New York).

Fowden, G., *The Egyptian Hermes* (Cambridge University Press, Cambridge, 1986).

Hanegraaff, W.J. (ed.), *Dictionary of Gnosis and Western Esotericism* (Brill, Leiden, 2005).

Luibheid, C., *Pseudo-Dionysius: The Complete Works*, an English translation (Paulist Press, New Jersey, 1987).

Mahé, J.-P., 'Les Définitions d'Hermès Trismégiste à Asclépius', *Revue des Sciences Religieuses* 50 (1976), 193-214.

Mahé, J.-P., 'La voie d'immortalité à la lumière des Hermetica de Nag Hammadi et de découvertes plus récentes', *Vigiliae Christianae* 45 (1991), 347-75.

Mahé, J.-P., 'Preliminary remarks on the Demotic Book of Thoth and the Greek Hermetica', *Vigiliae Christianae* 50 (1996), 353-63.

Mahé, J.-P., *'The Definitions of Hermes Trismegistus to Asclepius'*, an English translation, in *The Way of Hermes* (Duckworth, London, 1999).

Naydler, J., *Temple of the Cosmos* (Inner Traditions, Rochester, Vermont, 1996).

Naydler, J., *Shamanic Wisdom in the Pyramid Texts* (Inner Traditions, Rochester, Vermont, 2005).

Naydler, J., 'Plato, Shamanism and Ancient Egypt', in *Temenos Academy Review* (2006).

Nock, A.D. and Festugière, A.J., French translation and critical edition of the *Corpus Hermeticum* and *Asclepius* (Les Belles Lettres, Paris, 1991; first published 1946).

Pagels, E., *The Gnostic Gospels* (Penguin, Harmondsworth, 1990; first published 1979).

Paramelle, J. and Mahé, J.-P., 'Nouveaux parallèles grecs aux Définitions hermétiques arméniennes', *Revue des Etudes Arméniennes* 22 (1990-91), 115-34.

Paramelle, J. and Mahé, J.-P., 'Extraits hermétiques inédits dans un manuscrit d'Oxford', *Revue des Etudes Grecques* 104 (1991), 109-39.

Procter, E.E.S., *Alfonso X of Castile* (Clarendon Press, Oxford, 1951).

Quispel, G., 'The Gospel of Thomas Revisited', in B. Barc (ed.), *Colloque international sur les textes de Nag Hammadi (Québec 22-25 août 1978)*, (Québec 1981), 218-66.

Robinson, J.M. (ed.), *The Nag Hammadi Library,* English translation of Gnostic scriptures (HarperCollins, San Francisco, 1990; first published 1978).

Ross, Hugh McGregor, *The Gospel of Thomas*, an English translation (Watkins, London, 2003; first published 1987).

Salaman, C.F.A., Van Oyen, D., Wharton, W.D., '*The Corpus Hermeticum*', an English translation, in *The Way of Hermes* (Duckworth, London, 1999).

Terian, A., 'The Hellenizing school, its time, place and scope of activities reconsidered', in N. Garsoïan et al. (eds), *East of Byzantium: Syria and Armenia in the Formative Period* (Dumbarton Oaks Publishing Service, Washington, 1982).

Yates, Frances A., *Giordano Bruno and the Hermetic Tradition* (University of Chicago Press, Chicago, 1991; 1st edn, 1964).

Index

This index refers to the section numbers which appear in bold in square brackets in the translation.